THE TRAGEDY OF ARMENIA

The Tragedy of Armenia

A Brief Study and Interpretation

BY

BERTHA S. PAPAZIAN

*With an Introduction by Secretary James L. Barton, D.D.,
of the American Board*

THE PILGRIM PRESS

BOSTON   CHICAGO

COPYRIGHT 1918
BY BERTHA S. PAPAZIAN

THE PILGRIM PRESS
BOSTON

TO THOSE
WHO COUNTED HONOR ABOVE LIFE
THE ARMENIAN DEAD

FOREWORD

This little book springs from my desire to bring to the attention of my fellow Americans the claims upon our sympathy and support of a great little nation, which, at this critical moment of world history, is making a supreme effort for long-denied liberation. Armenia is known to us chiefly through her sufferings. With the other phases of her story we are largely unacquainted. To appreciate fully the justice of her appeal for complete emancipation, we should know more of her character and of the part she has played in the past, and in the present war. I shall be happy if this little book, in any degree, serves this end.

BERTHA S. PAPAZIAN.

Cambridge, Mass.
October, 1918.

INTRODUCTION

Armenian crucifixion at the hand of the Turkish Government and with the approval if not direct co-operation of Germany, has touched the heart of humanity. The world has witnessed one of the most ancient and notable of all the races of history subject to protracted attacks, atrocious beyond the power of words to describe, with no conceivable reason except to exterminate an entire people whose chief offence was industry and whose unforgivable crime the profession and practice of Christianity.

This story is the Armenian side of one of the tragedies of ancient and modern history, told simply, without passion and harrowing details, and yet with directness and pathos commanding our profoundest admiration.

It is one of the marvels of history that the Armenian nation, swept with almost perpetual war, persecution and massacre for many long dark centuries, has retained its beautiful language, its religion and its national soul, and now in these days of race redemption is ready to come into its own as a people worthy and capable of self-determination.

The Armenians, by their loyalty and devotion to the cause of the Allies in Russia, Turkey, Persia and Palestine, as well as in the armies of England, France and the United States, cannot, without most flagrant display of ingratitude, be ignored when the status of the lesser nations is decided.

Belgium, by her heroic resistance to the atrocious demands of Germany, saved Paris and made the world her debtor; so Armenia, refusing to cast in her lot with the Central Powers in partnership with Islam, stood loyal to the Allies and made it impossible for Germany to consummate her designs in the Caucasus and Eastern Turkey.

Serbia and Belgium have been martyr nations for four years, Poland and Bohemia for from one to three centuries; but Armenia has been in virtual bondage for a thousand years, during which period she has kept her home fires burning, her hopes undimmed and her soul unintimidated. Armenia lives today, although bleeding and stricken, because she was worthy. If this war ends and the final peace treaties are written and the Peace Congress dissolves without Armenia's obtaining her independence from Moslem rule with every opportunity for self-direction and self-expression in quietness and safety, then this war will in so far have been fought in vain.

We ask for the emancipation of Armenia from the rule of the Turk and the Russian, not because she has been for centuries enslaved, not because she has been afflicted as few other nations have suffered, and yet has persevered; not for pity or for sympathy's sake, but in the name of justice and inherent right to live as a free people. Tested in the furnace of the centuries of affliction, and weighed in the balance of national endowments, Armenians have demonstrated their inherent worth. From every point of view and measured by every standard of national capacity, they have a right to demand and expect the support of the Allies in their claims for national recognition.

This little book reveals the spirit and soul of Armenia, the depths of the longing of that ancient yet present living people, the height of their hopes and the earnestness of their purpose. We have been accustomed to think of the Armenians as a bleeding, stricken nation, and to them our sympathies have flowed in substantial expression. Let us now think of them as rising from the ashes of their persecution into a newness of life, and with their loyalty to the eternal principles of democracy, justice, righteousness and brotherhood established, let us heartily welcome them into the sisterhood of nations. America, which for nearly a century has labored for and suffered with them more than any other western nation, should be the first to champion their cause and pledge them its unchanging allegiance and support.

JAMES L. BARTON.

CONTENTS

		PAGE
	Foreword	vii
	Introduction	ix
I	Pagan Days	1
II	From the Conversion to the Crusades	18
III	Under Turkish Domination and the Spiritual Renaissance	41
IV	The Rise and Influence of the Near Eastern Question	58
V	After the Massacres	81
VI	In the World War	100
VII	In the World Court	128
	Notes	149
	Bibliography	159

THE TRAGEDY OF ARMENIA

Lift up thy head, weep not!   Holy is grief,
  And great and wholesome. Earth naught nobler knows
Than is the victim brave beneath his cross.
  'Tis in the shadow that the dawn-light grows.

The black destroyers, the red torturers
  Shall vanish — they like smoke shall disappear,
And from thine ashes thou shalt rise again,
  Made young by suffering, radiant, bright and clear.

. . . .

Thou shalt come forth triumphant from these shades;
  Stars shall thine eyes become, and sparkle bright;
Thy wounds to radiant roses shall be changed,
  And from thy whitened hair shall spring forth light.

Thou at the opening of the ways shall stand,
  And break the bonds that held thee down in gloom.
O Mother, rise! thy pains were childbirth pangs;
It is a world that stirs within thy womb!

—From the " Lullaby for Mother Armenia "
        By *Archag Tchobanian.*

(*Translated into English by Alice Stone Blackwell*)

The Tragedy of Armenia

Chapter I

PAGAN DAYS

ALTHOUGH these are the days of action rather than of reflection; although the hurried massing of millions of men and of billions of dollars, the building of immense docks and factories and railroads and hospitals and camps, of fleet upon fleet for sea and sky, the marshaling of labor, the organizing of huge civilian populations, the endless minutiæ of war, are taxing all the energies of mankind to the uttermost, there is, at the same time, an intensified thinking going on, often subconscious, but more incisive and compelling than any we have experienced in many a long year. The ethical and intellectual laws about which we had been feebly and abstractedly debating have suddenly become as imperiously real, as tangibly evident, as any demonstration in mathematics or physics. We know that the war we are witnessing, in spite of its overwhelming material manifestations, is nothing other than an immense moral upheaval; that it is the innermost become outermost; the word made flesh. And we are forced to recognize the irresistible power of Spiritual Law.

It is less difficult now than formerly to present the claims of far-away Armenia. As sharers in the same peril we are more ready to listen and consider. We dare not, as before, flee with the cry upon our lips, "This is too sad to talk about." We are eager to hear all. "The greatest tragedy in all human history" draws more and more near to us. Especially when we realize, as more and more we are coming to do, that this age-long agony, from even the contemplation of which the selfish world has shrunk, typifies in little the present tremendous conflict between Darkness and Light, and that it is the substratum and occasion, in a very real though indirect and negative way, of the world conflict.

To the tragedy of tragedies, only the Master Craftsman could have designed such a climax as this. A small and distant people, pitifully praying in the name of Liberty and Christianity for redemption from the foe of both, appealing in the midst of massacre and devastation to its treaty rights—what diplomat would believe that the neglect to heed could entail such stupendous consequences? What sovereign could foresee that as a result of mere callous disregard of moral and treaty obligations, a new sanction would be given to international treachery, a new impetus to the claims of tyranny; that the Kaiser would seize the opportunity to make common cause with the Sultan; that bargains would be struck to neutralize the peril of international interference, railroad concessions balancing against murdered human beings, and banking concessions against outraged womanhood, pillage, and arson; that pan-Islamic, pan-Turanian schemes would emerge into prospect, flattered by the encouragement of a European government which was in time to reject all Christian and democratic philosophy and to unite its creed of ruthlessness and brute force to that of the Turk, the ancient archenemy of all that we hold dear?

But the record is before us, and it is only

in the light of the world conflagration that we can learn its full import. All poetic justice seems blind when compared with the judgment which this light reveals. One reads in profound sorrow mingled with admiration for the heroic victims of this international bad faith, of these unscrupulous imperial designs, and with shame and reprobation in differing degree for the other protagonists. And, as the climax approaches, and stern retributive Justice enters and the fateful lightnings of her terrible swift sword enflame the whole world, even then the soul can but approve the awful sentence and exclaim: "Mine eyes have seen the glory of the coming of the Lord!"

One despairs of being able to summon the idea in all the force of its beauty and terror. One longs for images but none come except those, complex and majestic, which are created only through long contemplation of this magnificent and dolorous history. One is the more embarrassed in the task because, since those dread years of '95, '96, and '09, when hundreds of thousands of defenceless Armenian men, women, and children were slaughtered in cold blood and with complete impunity by the Turkish overlords, while responsible Europe looked passively on, and even humane but un-committed America seemed unable to interfere, the world has accepted Armenia as a static symbol of suffering. It has seen in her merely a figure with hands outstretched in useless supplication, and, except for the coin which it has given her for bread, it has passed on without other thought or reaction.

To envisage the tragedy as involving in its course the flow of the blood of all nations is, therefore, not only to give it its true political and moral bearing, but to reveal something of its own inherent Titanic grandeur. When the Editor of *The World's Work,* prefacing Ambassador Morgenthau's series of articles on "Two Years of War in Turkey," says: "Americans who wish to know why their sons are being transformed into soldiers can look to this narrative of events in the minaretted city on the Bosphorus," he indicates the power and sweep of the forces that have been there at work. With "Berlin to Bagdad" in mind as the slogan of the projected pan-Germania, the failure of the Powers to fulfill their treaty obligations to Armenia in the years '95 and '96, when the call most emphatically came for the decent solution of the Near Eastern question, becomes clearly an evasion of duty the most fate-laden in all history. And the aspirations and unaided struggles of Armenia assume, accordingly, a majesty and a significance absolutely unsurpassed.

But, unfortunately, both for us of America, and for the West in general, as well as for the Armenians themselves, the spiritual glories of this great national drama have been all but hidden from foreigners, except for the few, who, either because of direct contact with this people or some other incentive, have been led especially to that rich field of research which has to do with their extraordinary history. For in modern universal history they do not appear, their political identity having become lost in that of their ultimate conqueror. And as the Turk himself, until about the middle of the last century, was virtually ostracized from European civilization, the Armenians passed into an oblivion only the more complete. When, therefore, toward the end of the nineteenth century, they appeared before the world as the victims of cruelties and injustices indescribable and unredressed, it is not to be wondered at, perhaps, that their name should come to be regarded chiefly as one of most shocking hopelessness and dread.

But this indicated a generally thoughtless habit of mind. A prolonged national ordeal implies a great national soul, and ought in itself to have suggested the splendidly heroic calibre of the people and of their antecedent history. Not only as the victims of colossal wrongs, but as a force singularly noble and dynamic ought we to know this race,— one of the most ancient—which today in spite of oppression and persecutions that would either have tamed or annihilated one of less resolute fibre, is still, wherever possible, lavishing its remaining strength on behalf of an emancipated world!

We cannot find in history a parallel to this story. We turn to art for terms of comparison and find none except in the tragic Greek concept of Prometheus chained to the rocks and torn by vultures for having brought light to the world. Even the artistic imagination has never compassed so extended a panorama of undying aspiration and obstinate disaster. How inadequate is "Polyeucte," Corneille's suggestive embodiment of the purely religious side of the struggle! And yet it is to literary tragedy—to that of classic Greece—that the mind must hark back if it would find anywhere, though on an immeasurably slighter scale, a story told with an equally perfect symmetry, an equal concentration of interest, a terror and pity equally progressive.

For dramatic time, the tragedy is set amid the rolling centuries. For place, we have a stage unsurpassed in its grandeur and historic association. And for chief protagonists, an Aryan[1] people, independent, inquiring and original of spirit, adventurous, practical and liberty-loving, whom fate leads beyond the frontiers of Europe and their brothers in blood to where the mighty headland of Asia is washed by the Black and Caspian seas.

Over twenty-five hundred years ago the actors entered the stage, little dreaming that they were treading soil destined to become "the most coveted highway of the world."

Before them as they marched eastward from Thrace, Thessaly, Phrygia, stood the great pinnacle of Ararat, yet to become a "memorial shaft" to millions of their martyred descendants. Snow-capped, towering seventeen thousand feet into the sky, it stood companioned by its sister peaks. In the general region were other mountains, among them the snow-crowned Varag. Encircled by some of these, upon the shoulders of the tableland, was the intensely blue salt lake of Van; and breaking from the mountain and hillsides were beautiful fountains and streams, and great rivers, two of which, the Tigris (ancient Hiddekel) and the Euphrates, Jewish history tells us, bordered the Garden of Eden.

But the legend of Adam and Eve, and of the Creator who walked in the Garden; the ark of Noah upon the peak of Ararat; the sojourn of Noah and his companions for some time upon the crest of Subhan Dagh—a strictly Armenian legend—these were to play their part in kindling patriotic imagination only at a later day. The first step was to maintain tribal integrity against the encroachments of surrounding despots. And, characteristically, the first episode in the national drama—it comes to us in a burst of idealized patriotic glory—is the victory of the freedom-loving Haig, the founder of the first Armenian dynasty, over the Assyrian tyrant, Bel.

A succession of many centuries followed, marked by the vicissitudes which are the usual lot of a border state, and during which indigenous tribes evidently became fused with the race of Haig, their great Aryan conqueror and chief. More and more extended grew the kingdom under a long line of kings of this Haikean dynasty until toward the beginning of the second dynasty, the Arshagoonian, under Tigranes the Great, it included Media, Assyria, Cilicia, and Phœnicia. To conflicts with Assyria, Babylonia, Media, Parthia, and Persia had been added conflicts with Macedonia and Rome. Again and again we see these mighty forces victorious, but only partially so. For the Armenians, though frequently overpowered, were never overcome. By statecraft, and by their remarkable power of assimilating their enemies no less than by force of arms, they continued to maintain their race and its traditions against all odds. Some innate and irresistible moral stamina enabled them to draw to their cause even the Persian satraps, Parthian princes, and Roman and Seleucian governors who at times ruled over them. Under such suzerainty, they often gathered strength to rise against the old or against some new oppressor, who, bent upon the conquest of Europe or of Asia, swept the country from east to west, or from west to east.

But war with Rome, instigated, during a period of unprecedented strength and glory, by the Parthian king, Mithridates, the father-in-law of Tigranes; wars between Parthia and Rome and between Rome and Persia were to reduce still further the Armenian dominion to the intolerable position of a strictly buffer state. It became a perpetual battle ground, now tributary to Rome, now to Parthia; but even when thus tributary, Armenian leaders of royal and ancient clans or houses, the Ardzrounians, the Pagratians, the Seunians and others, struggling independently both against their would-be masters and against outlying states, succeeded not only in maintaining the standard of Armenian independence, but even in establishing new principalities. And as the political power waned, the national character became more and more clearly defined and the longing for a truly national life more intense.

In the kaleidoscopic pageant of these turbulent centuries, the stage is peopled with mighty historic figures. Confronting Haig, Aram, Ardashes, Ara, Tigranes and the other Armenian kings, are Bel, Tiglath-Pileser, Sardanapalus, Semiramis, Cyrus, Darius, Alexander the Great, Mithridates, Sulla, Crassus, Pompey, Mark Antony. Abroad, we see the Armenian king and his followers at the siege of Troy, on the side of Priam, or at Nineveh, at its fall; or, in less fortunate days, against a background of torches and garlands, we see him kneeling— a vassal king—to receive the crown from Nero in the area before the palace at Rome; or we see him captive, fettered with golden chains, a token of his own triumph which Mark Antony sent to Cleopatra.

In the politico-social life of this extended

period, we catch glimpses of other dramatic figures: as prisoner of war, "a noble Hebrew prince, Shempad by name" who affiliated himself with his conquerors, and became the founder of one of the royal households; the sons of Sennacherib who, after having assassinated their imperial father, "escaped into the land of Armenia," were received by the court and married Armenian princesses; and Hannibal, who fleeing from the vengeance of Rome, took refuge first with Antiochus of Seleucia, and then with Ardashes of Armenia for whom he drew the plan of the city of Ardashat.

Fortified castles of oriental splendor, citadels, towered walls, laden caravans and river argosies, market places, caravanseries, temples to the gods—to those of Persia and Greece and other foreign countries as well as to those of Armenia—make up the shifting background of the scenes. For both through the foreign conquests imposed upon her, and through her own commercial genius, the nation is in contact with and is at school to the world. The costumes of the characters are vivid; especially do we hear of this during the reign of Tigranes, when the dress of the period is described as "beautiful enough to transform even the most ugly." This, of course, refers to that of the favored classes, who also, men as well as women, wore heavy gold chains and necklaces and "rings of gold in their ears." The king wears now a wreath of pearls, or a crown set with immense rubies, placed upon his head by one of his own Pagratian nobles, who alone enjoyed this privilege; or again the crown and purple of Rome as in the days of Antoninus Pius, who sent these tokens of royalty to the Armenian king by special embassy. Even the pages of the royal households wear "rich vestments." There is much use of fur. The costumes of the military officers and soldiery add to the color of the picture. In the days of Herodotus "their arms are like those of the Phrygians." They wear helmets of laced leather and carry spears and shields. Later we see them in iron armor, charging magnificently upon the horses for which their country was famous, and which enabled the Armenian soldiery to become "the best cavalry in the world."

In the temple schools, religious and ritualistic lore is taught, and on the tablets in the temple libraries are the archives of priest and king for the enlightenment of patriot and scholar. A multitude of cults claim each its votaries. As the people come under the sway now of Macedonia, now of Rome, now of Persia, each tries to impose upon them her own particular culture. The reflective and cosmopolitan mind of the race is turned upon the thought of each, even while the basic allegiance to national tradition is being fostered popularly by the bards—especially those of Coghtn, a locality famous alike for its minstrels and its vineyards—who go from castle to castle and from festival to festival singing the cosmic myth of the old Armenian sun-god, Vahakn, or the more human romances of love and battle which marked the lives of the ancient kings. From the lips of these singers the people learn of the frightful dragons slain by the early heroes, the dragon being their symbol for mighty enemy nations. They hear, too, of the generous largess of their own kings, in the songs which recount glowingly that it "rained gold when Ardashes became King," and that the "pearls fell in showers when Queen Satenik became a bride."

Banquets, too, in honor of the gods; great festival days which bring the people to the groves of sacred poplars by the leaves of which the priests divine; or to the banks of the rivers where white horses and cattle are offered to the waves; to the fêtes champêtres on Navasard, the New Year, when libations are poured to Aramazd; or to the temples where flocks of doves are loosed and roses strewn in honor of the goddess Anahit,—all these festivals and ceremonials serve to unite the people, to develop the national consciousness, to engender what Tchobanian calls "the love of the race for itself."

But the racial soul, though preserved and differentiated through centuries of struggle and at the cost of immense suffering, is none the less, by the first century of our era, seemingly in solution. Natural inclination as well as force of circumstances are drawing the people unconsciously but irresistibly toward the culture of the Romans, and of the Greeks, their one-time congeners of Thrace and Thessaly. But Persia, their formidable eastern neighbor, has also a noble culture and an inflexible will to conquer, and it would seem unavoidable, and therefore the part of wisdom, to yield much to her.

A higher destiny, however, awaited the Armenians. Neither to the Romans nor to the Persians were they to surrender their spiritual identity. The vision of a new order was to take possession of their souls—an order differing religiously, socially, and politically from any that had preceded it. It was a moment fraught with worlds of how much significance and peril, when, at the dawn of the Christian era, politically in vassalage to Pagan powers, the race turned its eyes toward Judea.

Chapter II

FROM THE CONVERSION TO THE CRUSADES

THE nature and significance of the Christian phase of the Armenian struggle is mirrored in the gigantic conflict which is going on before our eyes today. It is, and has been, chiefly, an aspect and a continuation of the terrific combat which threatened to annihilate Europe at the time of the Mohammedan invasions. It is the conflict of two irreconcilables: the philosophy of Christ with its inherent democracy and its progressive implications, its divine discontent, and that of Islam—especially of Turkish Islam— with its autocratic and fatalistic leanings. And this, of course, is the fundamental issue of the present struggle. The fact that German "iron crosses" figure on the side of the enemy; the fact that the German deification of Force and of the Sword goes by some other name in no way alters the identity of the issue. Teuton and Turk have united to evoke again the abhorrent vision of world conquest in the name of a God of Battles. Had the Mohammedans of India, Persia, China, Arabia, and Egypt responded to the Berlin-Constantinople invitation to rise in Holy War against the Christian world, we should now be experiencing the full truth of this statement in all its devastating import.

The Armenian phase of this struggle of ethically inspired democracy against theocratic absolutism covers a period of about fifteen hundred years. In the case of individuals and communities, it began even earlier than that, no doubt in the first century to which the Armenians trace the beginnings of their martyrology, in the person of the Princess Santoukhd. The establishment of Christianity as a national religion by King Tiridates, in the year 301, suggests a long antecedent development of the faith among the people in general, and the usual price in suffering. But this is partly a matter of civil history. Exclusively religious wars do not appear to have occurred until some time after the official conversion, although a conflict of this sort is recorded in the year 232, with

Ardashir of Persia as instigator. And in the year 311, because of its religious beliefs, the nation had incurred the hostility of Rome to such an extent that, according to Eusebius, the Emperor Maximianus declared general war upon it. This particular disaster was, however, averted by the accession of Constantine to the throne.

With the bare fact of a Christianity ineradicable from the people, and for which they have suffered greatly, we are all more or less familiar through the later stories of Turkish persecution. But it is a fact which has lost rather than gained because of a too casual iteration. In centuries dominated by commercial considerations—like the beginning of the present, and the past—it had no practical weight whatever. As an incentive to armed intervention on their behalf, we know that it utterly failed, Christianity as a rallying point, or as an inspired conviction and rule of life, having everywhere lost its force in the West.

But circumstances have helped to make of Armenia the unceasing champion of this stupendous cause. Among nations she is the mother of Red Cross knights *par excellence*. Persecution has only increased her fidelity and her courage and clarified her vision. Proximity and subjection to anti-Christian rule have enabled her to estimate properly the menace of this sovereignty. And even as she has struggled against it throughout her history, so has she warned Europe of its danger and invoked her aid.

To understand her story we must therefore re-orient ourselves with regard both to the idea "Christianity," and to the idea "tragedy" of which Christianity has been in large part the occasion. We must cease to see in them mere fortuitous circumstance. It was the heroic adoption and defence of an exalted life principle which has brought the Armenians so much suffering. And the consequences are not to be regarded as meaningless disaster, but as genuine tragedy in the classic sense: a doom fashioned for itself, in large measure, by high and exceptional character through uncompromising devotion to some great end.

Let us remember, first, that the pioneer adoption of Christianity by the Pagan Armenian state was a consciously creative act, and that it required more hardihood, originality and hospitality of mind than was involved in the adoption of this religion after it had received the sanction of Rome and Byzantium. It was, in fact, a more momentous step than that which had led their ancestors to leave their European brothers and strike out across the highlands of Asia; although it signified in the realm of ideas something of the same capacity for adventure and leadership. And shortly this tendency was to receive further illustration along still other moral lines.

It is worthy of note that the Armenian church which St. Gregory founded and King Tiridates proclaimed some years before the proclamation of Constantine, was to remain an *independent* church, in spite of persistent overtures from both the Roman and Greek churches, and the practical advantages which might naturally have accrued from alliance with either. Second, that it was to assume very early in its history a *democratic* character, the election of the Catholicos and other clergy by popular consent being one of its outstanding features. And third, that although originally of an austere primitive simplicity, it soon appeared too ritualistic to a portion of this spiritually progressive people, for as early as the fifth century there appeared in Armenia a powerful and much persecuted Protestant sect, the Thonrakians, to the influence of which as it spread under various names through Europe, historians attribute the Reformation, and John Fiske, in his *Beginnings of New England*,[2] the Puritan movement which has moulded the character of our American institutions.

Thus we see this politically subject Aryan race whose lot was cast beyond the frontiers of Europe, expressing and applying what was later to become a distinguishing feature of the Western world: the right of the individual to be heard in matters civil and religious. "In politics they leaned toward Democracy," comments Fiske in writing of these early Protestants. One cannot imagine a more fatal circumstance than that which placed such a people in such an environment. Even had they been able to accommodate themselves to the idea of submission in religion and politics it would scarcely have solved their problem. There would still have remained the racial affinity which bound them to Europe and which at the time of the Crusades caused Melik Nasr, the Egyptian Sultan, to declare to Leo II, their king, who had applied to him for a treaty of peace: "I will never make peace with you until you promise on oath not to hold any correspondence or communication with Western nations." The bond at that time was not solely religious: it was also social and commercial. It was due to the instinctive sympathy of the people for their kin and for all that savored of progress. And even today this same spirit is making itself felt. At this very moment, poorly equipped and at the mercy of an absolutely pitiless foe, their influence in the Caucasus counts on the side of America and the Allies, and so it is in Mesopotamia, Palestine, France—wherever they are to be found. If there is an instance of similar ingrained constancy to heroic ideals under equally desperate conditions, history has not recorded it. May we not hereafter hear less of Armenia as victim and more of her as transcendent heroine?

To follow this story from the earliest Christian days to the time when the night of Turkish oppression settled upon the land is to traverse a period every whit as rugged and various, as picturesque and colorful, as were the most glorious days of the pagan era. If we pass over the trembling dawn of the Conversion and come to the fourth and fifth centuries, we shall see all over this still politically distracted period evidences of an intensification of the national spirit hitherto unexampled.

Although divided at this time between Persia and Byzantium, the people, rising as one in response to the new ideal, mustered abundant evidence of the strength of their moral and intellectual power. With an uncompromising zeal—much to be regretted from the historical and artistic points of view—they succeeded in virtually obliterating all traces of their pagan life and culture. But they created in its stead another civilization. The pagan temples, and the connecting libraries, so rich in the archives of king and priest that histories had previously been compiled from them, were regrettably demolished. Fire altars and the golden statues of the divinities met with the same fate. But upon the spot where, according to Neumann, had stood a statue of Hercules, there rose the Mother Church of Armenia, and a new and Christian art came into being. In the noble architecture which was evolved, scholars see the foreshadowing of the Gothic; in the music, poignant, austere, and characteristic, lies high evidence of esthetic power; but it is in the literature, which sprang into being almost miraculously, that we may most clearly see evidence of the fervid spiritual creativeness which the new life concept occasioned.

In this aspect of the drama is foreshadowed in intensified and triumphant form that intellectual activity and hunger which was to be characteristic of the Armenians throughout their subsequent history. To Rome, to Athens, to Byzantium, to Alexandria, flocked the mature scholars and the aspiring students, just as during the modern renaissance they were to flock to the European and American centers of learning. The Armenian alphabet was invented at this time, as a more fitting medium by which to transcribe the thoughts of the race than had been the foreign characters—Syriac, Greek, and Pelhevi—hitherto used by them. Great care was lavished upon the study of the Greek and Armenian tongues, and, as a result, the whole Bible had been incomparably translated from the Greek by the year 410, and the Golden Age of Armenian classic literature had begun. Moreover, the people had secured for themselves one of the greatest assets of national life,—a noble and subtle literary language. Referring to this movement, Dr. Dwight, the American Orientalist, says:

"Rarely have men in any age or country made more energetic, praiseworthy and successful efforts in the cultivation of letters than those whose names are recorded in the annals of Armenian literature during the fourth and fifth centuries. Their names are and will be deserving of the most honorable remembrance wherever real merit is appreciated and the love of letters cherished."

But Persia was viewing with increasing hostility this national awakening and *rapprochement* with Europe. Already, according to historians, she had entered into secret alliance with India against the so-called Western principle. She rightly estimated that the Christian and progressive tendencies of the new order would alienate the Armenians irrevocably from the pagan tyrannies. So she launched upon the country fierce religious wars, and, in the name of her King, Hazgherd, summoned Armenia to renounce Christianity and pay fealty to Ormuzd, and the principle of Fire. She flooded the country with her armies, and Armenia, though lacking a central government of her own, took up the challenge. She organized a "popular movement," a Holy League and army composed of the heads of the ancient houses and the bishops of the Church and their followers and retainers, and sent forth this great army of Christian knights to meet the hosts of Persia. Already she was practising democratic action. On her side these were peoples' wars.

On her spiritual victory over her first great religious foe there is not time to dwell. Suffice it to say that carnage and persecution only served to stamp the Christian ideal more ineffaceably upon the hearts of the people, and that in 451 on the memorable field of Avarair, Persia finally recognized the futility of attempting religious coercion. Meanwhile, Byzantium, from affiliation with whose church Armenia had separated at the Council of Chalcedon, had begun to prey more oppressively upon the harassed state where "two tides, that of the East and that of the West, strove for mastery." And so the civilization which the Armenians were developing received a sudden and serious check. But racially and religiously they withstood the onslaught, and, cheated of their political destiny at home, they sought in the service of their Byzantine foe and rival an outlet for their creative energies. And so victorious were they that according to Finlay, Bryce, Schlumberger, Rambaud, Bussell, Gelzer, and others, the Eastern Empire was for several centuries not Greek but Armenian. It was the Armenian Emperor Leo, known as the Image Breaker because of his iconoclasm, who commanded Rome to destroy her images. He had been converted by the

Armenian Paul, to whom the Protestant sect of the Paulicians owes its name.

But the most important event in connection with this peaceful conquest of Byzantium was the service which it enabled the Armenians to pay to Western civilization. They filled the civil offices and officered the army, and Leo the Iconoclast was still emperor when the Saracens hurled against Constantinople the largest Mohammedan army ever assembled. "Of its 180,000 men, only 30,000 got back home, according to Mohammedan authorities," says Finlay, and he adds: "Twenty-two years later, Leo annihilated another great Moslem army, and for two centuries the Saracens scarcely troubled the empire again." By this service, as momentous as was that of Charles Martel upon the field of Tours, the Armenians have placed the entire world in their debt.

Meanwhile, in Armenia proper, we see the nation again rallying incredibly under a third dynasty of their own kings, the Pakradoonian, with Ani, the city of a thousand churches, as its capital. But we see, too, the old jealous Destiny at work. The Greeks, who had again gained the ascendancy in Byzantium, warred upon this kingdom ceaselessly, actuated partly by their hostility towards the independent Armenian Church; and, finally, leaguing themselves with the Saracens, they compelled it to surrender (1045).

And so the third Armenian dynasty fell, after an existence of three hundred years; and so were frustrated, as so often before, the efforts of the Armenian race to realize in freedom its own genius. Of the monuments which remain of this civilization, Lynch says that "they throw strong light upon the character of the Armenian people and bring into pronouncement important features of Armenian history," that "they denote a standard of culture far in advance of the contemporary standard in the West," and that "they leave no doubt that this people may be included in the small number of races susceptible of the highest culture."

But Byzantium herself was to rue the fatal downfall of the Pagratids. Just as she was triumphing over their humiliation, there loomed upon the horizon great hosts of tribesmen from Mongolia and Tartary, as if in prophecy of the vengeance which should follow. Alp Arslan, the precursor of Genghis Khan, Ertoghrul, and Othman, suggested, could she but have read the lesson, the subsequent capture of her own capital city by Mohammed II and her own overthrow. In helping to destroy the Pakradoonian kingdom, she had shattered "the advance guard of Christian civilization in the East," and had opened the way to the invading foe.

With fate so much against them, the Armenians might now have retired from further contest and still, having survived the Assyrians, the Babylonians—and the Jews, upon the home ground—be reckoned a marvelously tenacious race. But they were not to retire. The old obstinacy of purpose, the old deathless courage of their ancestors still mastered them, and inspired certain feudal princes to still another attempt at establishing an Armenian state. One of these, Rhupen of the Mountain, a cousin to the Pakradoonian kings, set up, on the heights of the Taurus overlooking the Mediterranean, another Armenian kingdom, known both as the Kingdom of Lesser Armenia and as the Kingdom of Cilicia, and by open and definite alignment with Europe, proved anew the singular cosmopolitan bias, the keen political vision of the racial stock. Attacked, besieged by Arabs and Tartars, intrigued against and even warred upon by Byzantium, the Rhupenian dynasty maintained its existence for three hundred years, and shaped for itself a strikingly liberal policy. Armenians were sent to colonize in Italy. Italians were welcomed in Cilicia. Active commercial relations were entered upon between the two countries, the governmental administration was perfected, so that in the thirteenth century Marco Polo, who visited it, was able to report that it "was governed with much justice and economy," and that "the port, Payas, was the magazine of all the precious merchandise and of all the wealth of the Orient." And when the Rhupenian line failed for want of an heir, the nation, for political purposes, invited a Latin prince of the French family of Lusignan to occupy the throne.

The Crusades had early offered to this Kingdom a signal opportunity for open advocacy of the Christian faith which it was not slow to accept. Regardless of their material safety, conscious only of the fact that spiritually and intellectually their destiny converged with that of Europe, the Armenians allied themselves to the Christian forces throughout the entire period "by lending aid in men, in horses, in arms, in food, in council" and "by acting as guides in the desert." The part they played in these struggles may be gauged by the recognition offered them by the popes and emperors of the period. On the other hand, their own expectation of succor may be gathered from this 12th century poem by the Armenian Nerses, called the Gracious, one of the nation's greatest poets and saints. The translation was made by Miss Zabelle Boyajian of London:

THE CRUSADERS

> Once more God hither moves their course;
> With countless infantry and horse,
> As swell the waves towards the strand,
> Fierce and tempestuous, they land.
> Like sands that by the ocean lie,
> Or like the stars that strew the sky,
> They fill the earth where'er they go

And whiten it as wool or snow.
Their voice is like the northern wind,
Driving the storm-cloud from behind.
They clear the land from end to end,
The unbelievers forth they send,
Redeeming from such hopeless plight
All Christians held within their might.
Now in the churches cold and dark,
Once more shall burn the taper's spark;
And you, my sons, late forced to flee
To distant lands, afar from me,
Shall now return in chariots fair
Drawn by brave steeds with trappings rare.
And I shall lift mine eyes above
Beholding near me those I love.
My arms about you I shall fold,
Rejoicing with a joy untold;
And my black robes aside will lay
To dress in greens and crimsons gay.

But, alas, although the Armenians put their all to the test, they were to see the hosts of Islam triumph. Weaker and weaker grew European resistance until at last, abandoned by the West, and in a terrible isolation, moral and military, the knights of Armenia stood alone upon their mountain tops and watched the crusading hosts recede never to return.

The kingdom was obliged to surrender to the Sultans of Egypt, in 1375, and their last king was made captive. After his ransom by Spain, in vain did he go from France to England and from England to France, begging these countries to mend their quarrels, to return to their task of defending Western civilization. His sagacious council was unheeded. The barbaric hordes inundated Armenia—Major, Minor, and Lesser—and drew nearer and yet more near to Constantinople.

An interminable succession of pictures throng upon the vision during this second grouping of the tragedy. The pageantry of the classic era made vivid to us by the historian Egishe—the fortresses, the high seats of the palaces, the bridal chambers, the dining places with carven platter and other costly vessels of the table, the ushers by the door, the cup-holders at the festival, the flower gardens and vineyards, the hunting excursions, the councils of the bishops and princes, the heroism of the battlefields—all dissolve and in their place come the glories of the foreign service at Byzantium, the triumph and the defeat of the Kingdom of Ani and the brilliancy and eclipse of the Kingdom of Cilicia. The scenes are invested with all the romance and glamour of the medieval period of Europe. Feudal virtues and feudal excesses characterize the social life. Great houses clash with one another, betray one another, display vengeance and hostility as well as splendid generosity and superhuman courage. The mountain heights are bristling with battlements. Armies swarm in the defiles and on the plains. The whole period surges with activity.

And yet, amid all the political strife and discord, there is room for Art to make its wonderful way; not only that of the classic period already referred to, not only in the architecture of the Kingdom of Ani, or in the beautiful anthems, liturgy and formal literature of the Church, but in a wonderful lyric poetry which graced especially the medieval period, and in many fascinating forms of purely decorative art.[3] The lyrical poetry of medieval Armenia has been declared by Mr. Valery Brussov, a contemporary Russian authority, to be "among the treasures of the world," and the genius of her decorative artists is evident from the wonderful carvings in stone, wood, ivory, and metal which they have left. Old tombstones, croziers, walls, cups, exhibit a workmanship the spirit and technique of which has been the inspiration of similar work in Europe. To Armenia, too, the origins of cloisonné enamel are traced. A type of picture called by the Armenians "thought-work," and made by the application of bits of fabric of different colors upon a plain background, is said to have so delighted Botticelli that he introduced it to Italy and made use of the idea in church decoration. In days precarious but still irradiated by the "fighting chance" these offerings to beauty formed a significant part of the background of the changing scenes. And we infer from their presence human happiness and rapture, gaiety and love.

Among the myriads of characters who defile across the stage we dimly discern the apostles, Thaddeus and Bartholomew, and the Princess Santoukhd and other martyrs who offered up their lives in the first faint dawn of Christianity. We see Ripsime, the beautiful Roman virgin, and her companions, who, to escape the attentions of the Emperor Diocletian, "took refuge in the outskirts of the Armenian capital, Vagharshapat," only to enkindle the desire of King Tiridates, from whom she also fled, to be later captured and finally executed for her noble obstinacy; we see the great Illuminator, Gregory, we see warrior bishop, Puritan democrat, feudal lord, scholar, artist, merchant, emperor, soldier, Red Cross knight,—all of Armenian race. We see, in his olive wreath, the Armenian Varastad, victor of the last Olympian game; Prœresius, the rhetorician, to whom Rome erected a statue with the following inscription, *Regina rerum Roma regi eloquentiae;* and generals and statesmen who add glory to Byzantium. Harun al Raschid, Conrad of Wittlesbach, Raymond of Toulouse, Godfrey of Bouillon, Bohemond, Tancred, Frederick Barbarossa, Richard the Lion-Hearted, Saladin, give place before our eyes to the frightful forms of Alp Arslan, Genghis Khan, and Tamerlane. And, throughout, whether against Persian tyrant, Saracen, Mongol, or Turk, we see massed the solid legions of the Armenian people, who not only met the enemy valiantly on countless battlefields, but who, as martyrs to the ideals of Christianity and nationality, laid down their lives heroically, simply, and as a matter of course.

Chapter III

UNDER TURKISH DOMINATION AND THE SPIRITUAL RENAISSANCE

THE "noble singleness of feature" which marked the moral aspect of the preceding stages of the drama, persists with a growing majesty and poignancy in the final stages. The loss by the Armenians of every vestige of political and military power raises the plane of action to that of the naked spirit in battle with brute force, ignorance, materialism, intrigue and treachery. In a sense, it becomes an issue between one little unarmed nation and the world. And as the protagonists other than Turkey enter—Christian Europe, and, in a remote and non-official way, Christian America—the concentration of interest, expectation, suspense, terror, loathing, shame, disappointment, and pity, mount to heights of intolerable intensity. The striking elements of beauty which still remain are all but lost in a chaos of the revolting and the sordid, the disgraceful and heart-rending.

The pagan period of the drama was marked, it is true, by immense political and military contests and upheavals and by all the horrors of foreign invasions. But these were the lot of most peoples in the days of early martial society. And while, as Lord Byron said, "it would be difficult to find the annals of a nation less stained with crimes than those of the Armenians," still they gave and took with the rest to some extent, and under Tigranes, at least, became a really imperial power. And the very fact that as a people they survived the military inundations of the great Oriental tyrannies which obliterated so many of their neighbors, and that they succeeded in maintaining and developing a civilization of their own, tinges the ordeal with all the luster of triumph.

The second period, too, although marked by severe and continuous religious and political persecution and the destruction of the attainments of two comparatively long and successful dynasties, is still flooded with the glory of action and conspicuous achievement. In the Aryan Persians, as in the Romans and Byzantines, the Armenians could recognize ethnic similarity, and extract from these conquerors a kind of moral tribute in the way of a quasi autonomy. The Saracens—Arab or Egyptian—were likewise of a highly evolved racial type. And there was a possibility even here for reciprocal adjustments.

But the race to which they now fell victim were marauding nomads from Central Asia, possessing no culture of their own, and of an inferior mentality. Whatever religion they may once have followed they speedily discarded in favor of a corrupted form of Islam, in the sword-worshiping, world-conquering aspects of which they saw reflected their own basic instincts. The six centuries which have elapsed since their coming and the power which they have enjoyed, have only served to prove their brutality and their worthlessness as factors in civilization. Plunder, murder and rape were and still are their main incentives to action, and their iniquities and incompetence have been provocative of endless wars, of which the present holocaust is but the logical culmination.

During the first three or more hundred years of this domination, the Armenians as a people were practically blotted out from the annals of history. Europe, unable or unwilling to contest the supremacy of the foe in Asia, had turned from the blighted East to the wonders of her own renaissance, and, except for her terrific struggles with the Turk as he encroached more and more upon the heart of her own territory, lent no direct assistance to the beleagured frontier. In vain did the popes preach new crusades. Byzantium was allowed to fall almost unaided. Eastern Christendom, as such, was forgotten.

The last Armenian dynasty had surrendered to the Sultans of Egypt just seventy-eight years before the capture of Constantinople. If the greater power had been unable to withstand the assaults of the foe, if massacre was the lot of masses of the Greeks and servitude the destiny of the survivors, how must it have fared with this people who lacked any semblance of political cohesion, in the days when Mohammed II was turning churches into mosques, and threatening to feed oats to his horse from the high altar of St. Peter's?

Except for the inhabitants of certain mountain regions difficult of access—two of which, Zeitoun and Sassoun, retained a rough independence until the present war—the Armenians were subjected everywhere to the ravages of fire, sword, pillage, and enslavement. Then, as now, love of plunder rather than love of Islam was the motive which led the soldiers to these extreme excesses. Four-fifths of all the loot accrued to them; the remaining fifth went to the Emperor. Consequently all the inhabitants, high and low, were stripped of their possessions. Resistance was impossible.

But even while the people of the homeland were being massacred and enslaved, the Armenians of the Dispersion, it is well to remember, were continuing to play their immemorial part in the war between Liberty and Tyranny, Civilization and Barbarism. "In 1410," writes Tchobanian, "all the Armenian nobility [of Poland whither they had emigrated in the 11th century] fought with the armies of Ladislas Jagello, and in the battle of Grundwaldt contributed to the victory. [The war between Poland and Prussia]. In 1683, in the great war of the Austrians against the Turks, five thousand Armenian soldiers fought valiantly with King Sobieski at the gates of Vienna."

Meanwhile, in Turkey, amid the appalling domestic decadence, moral and material, which attended the barbaric reigns of the successive Sultans; under the terrific strain of constant and burdensome wars undertaken by the usurpers against Europe, Persia, and Egypt; scattered unarmed among a foe whose authority was swiftly and summarily enforced by the scimitar, by poison, by the rope, by strangulation, by imprisonment; a foe which took the savage's delight in devising new methods of torture, and which claimed religious sanction for all abominations inflicted upon the *Giaours* (infidels); amid this incredible orgy of license and cruelty, which, in the earlier days, had struck terror into the hearts of free and powerful peoples, the Armenians, with a tenacity as amazing as characteristic, gradually resumed in impressive, though in far humbler form, something of the old rôle of intellectual and practical leadership which at other times in their history had resulted in the conquest of their conquerors.

Banned from the army, their word refused in courts of law, the women subject to seizure, their property to confiscation upon no provocation, taxed to the utmost, they nevertheless succeeded in maintaining some kind of civil and social fabric for the wastrels who had overpowered them. They were the bankers, artists, traders, artisans, and farmers; but even as they conducted the commerce, plied the trades, tilled the fields, built the marble palaces, filled those administrative posts which demanded constructive ability, went as ambassadors to foreign countries, and in all ways augmented the resources of the State, they were, as a people, despised and outlawed by their idle and arrogant masters who looked upon them as *"rayahs"* fit only to be exploited; and in secret and in silence the noble traditions of their own race and religion took deep and deeper root.

During these centuries of enslavement, the Armenian race lost much by migrations, forced and voluntary. Europe, India, and Persia claimed the ambitions of many of the ablest. Evidence of the early Armenian dispersion in Europe is to be found in the fact that books in Armenian characters were printed as early as 1488 at Venice and Amsterdam, and at Lembourg, Milan, Paris, Marseilles, Leipzig, and Padua, during the years of the two succeeding centuries. They are said to have founded the city of Calcutta. Certain it is that they rose to wealth and influence in the life of British East India in general, and that they enjoyed privileges there usually reserved for Englishmen alone. We hear of them as "prime ministers" to the native princes; and as confidential servants to the British crown.

The songs of homesickness, or of longing for the emigrant, which appear at this time, testify to the sufferings and losses inflicted by these migrations. A melancholy settled upon the spirit of the people. It is felt in their music. It throbs in their poetry. "No Christian dare look a Turk in the face," commented a European traveler who was one of the first to cross the gulf which had separated the country from the West since the Turkish occupation. The scimitar and the bludgeon of the Turk had indeed overawed the defenceless Christian populations. There was no contesting the might of his brutal force.

But the Armenians had a higher daring. They alone, of all the peoples of Asia which had fallen beneath his yoke, had achieved the miracle of retaining the four great essentials of national life—racial purity, racial customs, religious integrity, and language. Even the soul of the once formidable Persia, which had been Mohammedanized by the Saracens, and which had come indirectly under Turkish influence, had lost its ancient characteristics. While the Chaldeans, the Ghebers, the Syrians, and, in Egypt, the Copts, had lost language, religion, or national traditions, one or more, the Armenians, on the contrary, not only jealously retained all their distinguishing features, but were to emerge at the end of the long struggle with a national consciousness distinctly heightened. This fact more than any other, says De Morgan, "entitles them now to a national re-birth."

The best that can be said of this period of bondage is that it taught the people endurance and reliance upon one another. Persecution brought the cohesion which their independent nature and the mountainous character of their country had tended to disrupt. Because of religious exclusiveness and sane habits of life they had suffered no racial degeneracy. Together with their intellectual vigor they had managed to retain their primitive physical strength. It was, on the whole, a fine race which had survived the conquest and captivity. Men and women there were of many types of form and of countenance; numbers tall and well knit, with faces of the distinctively Armenian cast:—lofty and, among the men, even massive foreheads, high noses, straight or aquiline, dark eyes, and hair abundant and black; their complexions and lips vivid with the rich color lent them by the brilliant sun and pure air of the great tableland and of the mountainous region of Cilicia; their demeanor grave and reposeful, reminiscent of the dignity of their neighbors of India. Others there were who showed traces of the Semitic strain which had mingled with the race during the dim days of the Babylonian captivity and at other periods of their history. Less repose but more vivacity marked their features. Not infrequently there appeared another type, more blooming but more delicate, of fairer and rosier skin, and more languorous air. And again it was not uncommon to see faces of a heavier cast which suggested descent from the tribes of the Kingdom of Ararat, the original Uradhu, which Haig had overcome. A similar variety one observes among all the European races.

These men and women had given to each other in monogamous marriage all those affections and loyalties which make family life devoted and high. Husband and wife, parents and children, sister and brother, stood by one another with a patriarchal simplicity and fervor. The children of the households were lovingly and wisely nurtured, and the old people honored. In their own homes and in their own churches they observed unnoticed their national and religious festivals. And in their own schools, which they themselves maintained, the more favored of the people received the education which their limited opportunities afforded. The knowledge of their past glories and of their ancient and medieval literatures were veiled from them, partly through the evolution of their language from the classic to the modern, partly through the scarcity of books, but more largely through the opposition of their masters to all that savored of enlightenment. The weight of the oppressor was so great and circumstances so hostile as almost to extinguish the aggressive intellectualism which has always been their dominant trait. Since the downfall of their last dynasty they had suffered all the crippling disabilities of a proscribed race. The production of a new literature was all but impossible.

But while body and soul were thus in bondage, the spirit of liberty and light which had guided the destiny of the race in other days was not without its testimony. Toward the close of the eighteenth century two great figures appear, one an incarnation of the political, the other of the cultural, genius of the Armenian race. It is evident through the career of Israel Ori that the dream of an independent Armenia had never completely faded, and that the fierce love of freedom which had characterized the feudal nobility had not wholly waned in their descendants.

Israel Ori was of Persian and not of Turkish Armenia, but his heroic scheme of political emancipation was intended to apply to all the Armenians who had come under the power of the tyrannical Mussulmans of the East. He was one of a group of Armenian *meliks* (hereditary princes) of the province of Karabagh, a mountainous district which, although paying tribute to Persia, had maintained a semi-autonomy. These men "yearned to enter upon a new era of freedom" and dared to take bold steps to secure that end. After repeated efforts at self-liberation the nobility of the rebellious principalities decided to send Ori as their representative to the courts of Europe with the object of soliciting the "aid and protection of the Powers," in the furtherance of the revolt at home. After twenty long years of unflagging effort, he finally succeeded in obtaining formal promises of help from the Emperor Leopold and Peter the Great. And although the outbreak of the Russo-Swedish war prevented the consummation of the project, the episode is none the less most significant in the life of the nation. It is more than a drama within a drama. It is part of the old sequence, and a prophecy of what was yet to follow. For we see foreshadowed in the patient but dauntless character of the chief actor, the patriots who were to plead the cause of their race so bravely and so steadfastly in the nineteenth and twentieth centuries.

The other great figure of this era of awakening is Mekhitar, an Armenian monk—a convert to Catholicity—who, realizing that he could accomplish nothing for his race should he remain in Turkey, left that benighted country for Venice, where, under the patronage of the Pope, he founded the great Armenian monastery and outpost of learning known as the Convent of St. Lazar. Here he and the brotherhood of Armenians whom he drew about him began their great work of editing and publishing the ancient works of the forefathers which they had brought with them in their ancient manuscript form. Here they wrote original histories and other books and compiled grammars and dictionaries. Here they translated the works of the writers of the Western world, of modern days and of antiquity. It was this movement which ushered in the sublime but ill-fated modern renaissance. Not only was knowledge of the deeds of the great kings who had gained for them nationality, and of the great saints who had brought them Christianity, made common property, not only were the splendid traditions of Ararat, Ani, and Cilicia revived; the mind of the people was brought into contact with the mind of Europe, and especially with that of France, so that by the middle years of the nineteenth century all the best modern theories and philosophies had their ardent votaries among these outcast subjects of the besotted and reactionary Ottoman State. Gradually the race very generally began to exhibit tokens of its old eager creativeness.

Other causes contributed to this awakening of the national spirit. The vivifying influence of Europe and America was felt in the persons of the statesmen, travelers, merchants and scholars, and—above all—missionaries and teachers who began to penetrate the country. Although these were of the race of the Crusaders, they knew nothing of these ancient allies of their forefathers, and were not prepared to meet a race so congenial of spirit, so dynamic and original of mind. "They are the Dutch of the East," wrote Dulaurier. "They are like the Swiss," said Lamartine. "We have found the Yankees of the East," exclaimed the American missionaries who had gone to the country for the purpose of converting the Mohammedan Turk.

Schools began to multiply, Armenian as well as American and French. The *rapprochement* with the West was further accelerated by the number of students, who, in the universities of Europe and America, at the Venetian monastery of St. Lazar, and at the sister house which had been established at Vienna, felt the divine flame of the rising civilization which their own ancestors had done so much to kindle and to foster. Not in the degraded concepts of Turkey, but in the visions of the aspiring West, did the Armenian spirit find fellowship and affirmation. It was evident that such a people could not longer endure the blighting limitations and exactions of the Turkish yoke.

Chapter IV

THE RISE AND INFLUENCE OF THE NEAR EASTERN QUESTION

THE modern Near Eastern Question was a weighty factor in the efflorescence of light and hope which revealed to the Armenians of the later nineteenth century all the degradation and horror of the Turkish domination, just as it was the chief force in the determination of the last, most terrible, and most piteous phase of the entire Armenian tragedy. In so far as it was concerned with the treatment of Christians in general, in the Near East, it was but a resumption of the ancient discussion begun by Charlemagne and Harun al Raschid. This has been a courtly, and, on the whole, a satisfactory correspondence, as were afterwards the interchanges between the Christian knights and the mighty Saladin. But the Turks were of another order, and the motives of the Western intercessors, too, had very radically changed.

The espousal of the Christian cause by

Russia, her assumption of the rôle of protector of the Christians of the East officially conferred upon her in 1774 by the Treaty of Kainardje, has, in spite of its obvious ulterior motive, something of the old chivalrous flavor of the Middle Ages. And this glamour of a semi-disinterested championship she somehow consistently managed to sustain until the coming to power of the reactionary Alexander III. In the face of her actual accomplishment and the fact that the wars she waged time after time on behalf of the Balkan Christians brought her no substantial increase in territory, we can hardly say that her motives were unmitigatedly sordid. We must make some possible allowance for Russian mysticism and ideality, and admit the possibility of a rude Christian *esprit de corps* in this uncouth nation, so late in coming under the "rationalizing" influence of the West. Or, even if we must suspect that her motives were always wholly selfish, we are obliged to admit that they none the less served most excellent ends.

However this may be, the revival of interest in the forgotten East on the part of the other

European powers was nothing if not frankly utilitarian. It is certain that they did not even play at dragon-killing. From the first, they recognized the iniquities of Turkish rule, especially as it affected the subject Christians, but they took no more than an academic interest in the matter. They had outgrown mysticism and sentimentality, and had become out and out opportunists, at least so far as foreign policies were concerned. With economic and territorial expansion as the guiding governmental motives, it was natural that the point of view of the Crusader should give way to that of the adept in diplomacy, the broker, the militarist. Especially after the first quarter of the nineteenth century did the relation between the West and the Turkish empire take on the definite character of a politico-economic gamble. Neither the religion nor the national aspirations of the Christian races were of any moment in the eyes of the great imperialisms, whatever these might mean to the more idealistic men and women of the respective home populations.

A corresponding change of outlook had not occurred among the Christians of Turkey.

There the issues of Christianity and of Nationality were still keen and vital, and the love and longing for freedom in these important respects were still intense because of centuries of denial on the one hand, and of valiant affirmation on the other. Besides, the Christians of the East, even the Armenians, although in the earlier days of their history as noted for their commercial genius as were the Phœnicians, and, in their later days, as are the Anglo-Saxons and the Jews, were practically untouched by that scientifically relentless commercial spirit of the Mechanical Age which had transformed Europe. Even the shrewdest bankers and business men were unsophisticated and primitive in their outlook when compared with this new type of financier and statesman which was evolving in the West and which reckoned personal and national profits in terms of politico-economic exploitation. Their dreams of liberation were founded upon quite another and simpler scheme of life.

Moreover, the masses of the Armenian people were farmers and tradesmen,—practical, frugal, shrewd, but, strange as it may seem, simple, and, in spite of a subtle native discernment, confiding. They idealized Europe. They respected her as a co-religionist, and admired her as the exemplar of Progress and establisher of Law. In spite of themselves, they could not help looking to her for ultimate redemption. The fact that the prophets and peoples of Europe and the narrow governing circles were two distinct propositions, neither the Christians of Turkey-in-Asia nor those of the Balkans seem ever fully to have grasped. In the Armenian struggle, this vain but persistent hope of a chivalrous European intervention adds the crowning torture to the culminating disasters which were to overtake them with almost annihilating force.

So much for the new factors which entered to complicate an already involved and desperate situation. On its political side, the contest resolved itself into a question either of the control or dismemberment of Turkey by one or more of the European powers or her own self-redemption. Her own corruption and incompetence, largely, had fashioned the *impasse*. Naturally, as an integral part of Turkey-in-Asia, the Armenians were chiefly concerned with internal reform. Unlike the Balkan nationalities, with them, as Viscount Bryce remarks, "The alternative to an Ottoman State was not an Armenian State, but a partition among the Powers, which would have ended the ambitions of Turk and Armenian alike. The Powers concerned were quite ready for a partition, if only they could agree upon a division of the spoils. This common inheritance of the Armenians and the Turks was potentially one of the richest countries in the Old World, and one of the few that had not yet been economically developed. The problem for the Armenians was not how to overthrow the Ottoman Empire but how to preserve it, and their interest in its preservation was even greater than that of their Turkish neighbors and co-heirs. . . . Talent and temperament had brought most of the industry, commerce, finance and skilled intellectual work of Turkey into the Armenians' hands. And if the Empire were preserved by timely reforms from within, the position of the Armenians would become still more favorable, for they were the only native element capable of raising the Empire economically, intellectually and morally to a European standard, by which alone its existence could permanently be secured."

Consequently, the Armenians were bent upon securing such reform. The constitution drawn up in '76 by the Armenian statesman, Krikor Odian, Secretary to the Turkish reformer, Midhat Pasha, which was proclaimed and then immediately revoked by Sultan Abdul Hamid, would have served this end. But the Government, blind to its own interest, and radically unable to see the legitimacy of reform demands—especially as they affected Christians—persisted in its suicidal policy of oppression. After every such demand it became more cruel and reactionary than ever.

However, there is a certain inexorable law, made axiomatic by the great Irish liberator, O'Connell, which we must not lose sight of. When all is said, we know that in exigencies of this sort "he who would be free, himself must first strike the blow." And we are likely to inquire if, other than by an occasional humble protest or petition, the Armenians of these modern days in any way proved themselves worthy to be ranked with the other heroic peoples—the Greeks, the Serbs, the Rumanians, the Bulgarians—who through storm and stress had been partly the means of effecting their own liberation from the Turkish yoke.

Considering that from the beginning of the Turkish domination the Armenians had never been permitted to bear or to possess arms; considering that they were widely scattered among watchful Turkish and Kurdish populations, it is by no means a fair question. Still, it is well for us to realize that in spite of these formidable handicaps—and aside from the so-called "revolutionary" movement, undertaken only as a last resort, and then with the desperate understanding that only by the help of Europe could it in any way avail—the Armenian race, owing to the genius and courage of a number of its own sons in the service of Russia, did actually secure a virtual emancipation from the most intolerable of their wrongs, but that the fruits of this victory were deliberately destroyed by the very Powers to whom they had most right to look for sympathy.

It was the Russo-Turkish war of '76-'78 which brought to the Armenians this opportunity. At the beginning of the century a portion of Armenia proper, the Caucasian district, had come under the dominion of the Czar. And the people thus freed from Turkish toils sprang to a height of material and moral prosperity sufficient to prove the artificial nature of their retardation in the interior of Asia Minor. Macler, De Morgan, Lynch, Bryce, all testify to the economic development of the region which they inhabited, once they had obtained even a measure of freedom. De Morgan states that under their hands the province became within a comparatively few years one of the most prosperous in all Russia.

But more significant even than this demonstration of economic power was the moral flowering of the people. Stimulated by their own liberties, by study in the Russian universities, and by contact with Russian, German, and French thought, the race produced a succession of patriots, warriors, thinkers, dramatists, novelists, and poets, of whom any race on earth might be proud. Europe, and especially France, is coming to know—largely through the efforts at Paris of Mr. Archag Tchobanian and Professor Frédéric Macler, professor of Armenian at *L'Ecole des Langues Orientales Vivantes*—something of the genius of this galaxy of writers. And the English-speaking world, through the labors of Miss Alice Stone Blackwell, Miss Zabelle Boyajian, Mr. Robert Arnot and others, is coming to know something of the poetry. But, as a potential factor in the life of the nation, no Armenian figure of the Caucasus can claim anything like the significance which invests the person of Loris Melikoff, confidante and advisor to Alexander II, who, with other Armenian generals, constituted the High Command of the Russian army on the Caucasian front in that momentous war.

The Turks were superior in numbers to the Russians, but, under the inspired direction of those men who felt that they were defending the old home ground, they were so decisively repulsed as to be constrained to comply with the vigorous but not ungenerous terms dictated to them by Russia in the Treaty of San Stefano. When we remember that Melikoff was yet to draft a constitution for Russia—which Czar Alexander was on the eve of proclaiming at the time of his assassination—that he was statesman as well as general, and that he was the greatest figure of the victorious war, we can easily recognize the influence of his hand in the sixteenth article of the Treaty of San Stefano which, under strong military guarantee, assured redemption to the Armenians of the scandalously misgoverned interior provinces.

The Article follows:

"As the evacuation by the Russian troops of the territory which they occupy in Armenia, and which is to be restored to Turkey, might give rise to conflicts and complications detrimental to the maintenance of good relations between the two countries, the Sublime Porte engages to carry into effect, without further delay, the improvements and reforms demanded by local requirement in the provinces inhabited by the Armenians, and to guarantee their security from Kurds and Circassians."

This, of course, meant that not until the reforms had been consummated would the

Russian troops be withdrawn. It was the first serious attempt that had been made by any European power on behalf of the Armenians, although such reform had been stipulated under the general heading "Christian" in the Treaty of Paris, and had at times since been the subject of international discussion. That the conditions demanded such drastic intervention is more than apparent from such testimony as that of C. B. Norman, then war-correspondent for the *London Times,* and numerous other foreign eye-witnesses:

"In my correspondence to the *Times,*" Mr. Norman writes, "I made it a rule to report nothing but what came under my own personal observation, or facts confirmed by European evidence.

"A complete list it is impossible for me to obtain, but from all sides . . . I hear piteous tales of the desolation that reigns throughout —villages deserted, towns abandoned, trade at a standstill, harvest ready for the sickle, but none to gather it in, husbands mourning their dishonored wives, parents their murdered children, churches despoiled and desecrated, graves dug up, young of both sexes carried off, and the inhabitants of villages driven naked into the fields, to gaze with horror on their burning homesteads."

There was but a brief moment, however, in which to rejoice and thank God for this long-sought deliverance promised by the Treaty of San Stefano. Hardly was their protection assured when England, already long committed to the so-called "integrity of Turkey" policy in the interests of her own Eastern possessions, promptly interfered and demanded that the treaty drawn up by Russia be revised at an International Convention. Already, she had sent her fleet through the Dardanelles in threat of war should Russia insist upon following up her successes. Russia was in no position to take up the challenge, so she submitted to England's dictation. The Treaty of San Stefano was annulled and that of Berlin substituted. The fruits of the well-earned victory of the Russians were effectively minimized. Incidentally, Melikoff's signal triumph on behalf of his people was turned to black defeat. More vulnerable than ever they had been in all their history, the all but liberated Armenians were handed back to their infuriated tormentors.

Still there remained a hope. By the 61st article of the Treaty of Berlin—secured chiefly through the efforts of an Armenian delegation headed by the ex-Patriarch Khrimian—the Six Great Powers, England, Germany, Austria, France, Italy, and Russia, had agreed to become the protector of the Armenians, although without any definite military guarantee.

The Article read:

"The Sublime Porte undertakes to carry out, without further delay, the improvements and reforms demanded by local requirements in the provinces inhabited by the Armenians, and to guarantee their security against the Circassians and Kurds. It will periodically make known the steps it has taken to this effect to the Powers, who will superintend their application."

Almost simultaneously, in secret conference with the Turkish Government, England had negotiated the Cyprus Convention, a treaty designed to secure both her own and Turkish interests against the further advance of

Russia. As one of the series of state documents which bear most strongly upon the destiny of the Armenians it deserves to be cited here. I quote the main article:

"If Batoum, Ardahan, Kars, or any of them shall be retained by Russia, and if any attempt shall be made at any future time by Russia to take possession of any further territories of His Imperial Majesty the Sultan in Asia, as fixed by the definitive Treaty of Peace, England engages to join His Imperial Majesty the Sultan in defending them by force of arms.

"In return, His Imperial Majesty the Sultan promises England to introduce necessary reforms, to be agreed upon later by the two Powers, into the government and for the protection of the Christian and other subjects of the Porte, in these territories; and in order to enable England to make necessary provision for executing her engagement His Imperial Majesty the Sultan further consents to assign the Island of Cyprus to be occupied and administered by England."

Thus Russia was ousted from her position as special protector of the Christians of the East, and Europe collectively and England particularly assumed responsibility for the execution of reforms in Armenia.

Once the Russian forces were withdrawn, the

Sultan, as might have been expected, immediately began to inaugurate a policy of reprisals which had for its aim nothing less than the total impoverishment and final extermination of the Armenian population. He rightly discounted the sincerity of Europe with regard to the Armenians, and decided to eliminate this element whose presence and whose status necessitated reform and might later offer further pretext for foreign intervention. The first and most conspicuous step to this end was the organization into regular cavalry of the marauding Kurdish tribes, from whose depredations the Armenians had especially been promised protection. These were given power over their lives, honor and property. Then, taxes already unbearable were increased and ingeniously multiplied; travel, even from town to town for business purposes, was virtually prohibited; the collection of debts from the non-Christian population was made impossible; imprisonment without trial and the open or secret murder of the leading men became common practices; the abduction and violation of women were encouraged and connived at by the officials.

Mrs. Isabella Bird Bishop, the famous traveler, who visited Armenia in 1890, gives this report of the conditions prevailing at that time:

"On the whole," she says, "the same condition of alarm prevails among the Armenians as I witnessed previously among the Syrian (often called Nestorian) *Rayahs*. It is more than alarm, it is *abject terror,* and not without good reason. In plain English, general lawlessness prevails over much of this region. Caravans are stopped and robbed, travelling is, for Armenians, absolutely unsafe, sheep and cattle are being driven off, and outrages, which it would be inexpedient to narrate, are being perpetrated. Nearly all the villages have been reduced to extreme poverty, while at the same time they are squeezed for the taxes which the Kurds have left them without the means of paying."

In vain in the midst of this reign of terror did the representatives of the people appeal over and over again to the Government for relief and redress. Finally, when it became only too evident that they were the victims of a vindictive design, they turned to the

Signatory Powers on the basis of their Berlin Treaty rights. That they were justified in doing this is evident from the official testimony of the foreign consuls and ambassadors in innumerable Blue and Yellow books, from the protesting speeches delivered in the European, and especially in the English and French parliaments, and from the representations which the Powers made to the Porte.

But, as we know, the Sultan, an adept in intrigue, took advantage of the jealousies of the Powers and played one off against the other while he continued his murderous policy with regard to the Armenians. There remained to the latter but one desperate chance. Some of the young men of the nation—many of whom had received their ideals from the prophets of Europe and America—organized themselves into patriotic societies for the sole purpose of self-defence. They managed to get possession of arms and were able successfully here and there to resist the outrages and depredations. Only thus, they had been told, might they win the respect and attention of Europe and secure her intervention.

We know what followed. The great massacres of '95 and '96 are still fresh in our minds. The tears for those unpunished crimes are yet upon the cheek, the shame is yet upon the brow, the agony is yet keen in the hearts of the great army of men and women of all races and nations who longed to arrest the murderous debauch but lacked the power to do so. The hills and valleys of the great tableland, the cities of the plains and of the sea coasts, even the capital city itself, dotted with foreign embassies, became the scene of a colossal butchery. In regions made sacred by the heroic defence of the Christian faith by this nation, its earliest adherent, the savage Turk was allowed to work his abhorrent will unchecked. The weaponless populations were visited with horrors which mankind had thought outgrown.

But while the funeral pyre of a nation was being kindled; while a humanity which had flowered nobly in spite of insuperable difficulties was being thrown as dross into the flames by barbaric and sacrilegious hands; while white-haired men and women and those filled with all the energy of their best years,

—fathers, mothers, brides, youths, maidens, and the angelic forms of little children who had but opened their trusting eyes upon this world,—were being sent to swell the hosts of martyrs to Christianity and to Freedom, the old frenzied cry of "Christ or Mohammed" ringing in their ears; upon the heights of old Zeitoun and amid the cliffs of Sassoun, where the race had preserved a scant immunity from Turkish power, there thundered forth the defiant voices of the ancient heroes in the shouts of the brave mountaineers, who, scantily armed, held the foe at bay for months to the marvel of the world.

Zeitoun, a hill town of the old Rhupenian dynasty, refused to surrender until formal peace terms had been entered upon by Turkey, at the instance of the foreign ambassadors. And when at Sassoun the inevitable happened and the Turks came rushing up the heights, the women of the villages, with their babies in their arms, calling upon God to accept them as sacrifices, hurled themselves from the precipices rather than fall into the debasing hands of the foe. And, on the plains, the mother river, Euphrates, received other hundreds of women and maidens who, guarding their integrity as the pearl of greatest price, flung their bodies to her rescuing waves.

It is no longer possible to summon up the individual forms which crowd the stage. The drama has burst its national bounds and has become world wide, even cosmic in its character. We see two worlds, one of darkness and one of light, struggling for birth in the hearts and minds of men. The gigantic evils embodied in a succession of depraved sultans and temporizing world policies, made manifest by this great crisis, present issues and opportunities which call for potent and colossal heroes. But we see none. The aged Gladstone's Cassandra-like warning, *"To serve Armenia is to serve Civilization,"* evokes no response, except among those who, in individual capacity—like the noble American missionaries and other humanitarians—take up the great burden of terror and agony as if it were their own, and harbor, comfort and watch with the people, or, before the governments and peoples of the world, cry out the story in all its shame and pity.[5] And even them we cease to see.

In this moment of stupendous cataclysm, when the fate not only of the Armenian nation, but of Civilization itself was trembling in the balance, while yet the nations had the power to deal the death blow to the power of Autocracy which was yet to ravage the world, it is as if the spirit of the Armenian nation, the prescience of these things and of the death of all her children upon her, took tangible form. We seem to see her rise with all her glorious past upon her. We see her turn horrified, dumbfounded and appealing eyes upon the six mighty Powers who had promised to aid her. She, the Apostle of Christianity, and its servant and defender, she, who had held back the Saracens in the days of her power, and had given of the might of her sons to the cause of the Crusades, she, a mother of Democracy, we see standing with bare, bleeding, outstretched hands in supplication to those children of the West,—the Six Great Knights, armed to the teeth, whose navies ride at will the oceans of the world, whose armies patrol the earth. We see her standing thus. But their great forms have become dwarfed, futile. Their eyes are averted; their ears deaf.

And then, her despairing eyes full of wild pleading, we see Armenia turn to America, to that fair Galahad among nations with the glory of his own great crusades for liberty still lighting his frank brow; to America, so friendly, so hospitable, so practiced in brotherhood, so determined to trample the evils inherited from the Old World and to develop and add to all the good; whose spirit had visited her land and had created oases whither the hunted souls and bodies of her children had found comfort and refuge. Armenia in that awful moment looks into his beautiful face. She sees the young eyes appalled at the sight of her great suffering; she sees the generous hands extended full of bounty; but she notices that though the scars of battle are upon his face, though the passion for justice is in his eyes,—the consciousness of his great mission has not yet fully dawned,—the knight is but an adolescent whose moment to enter the world's lists has not yet arrived.[6]

Chapter V

AFTER THE MASSACRES

FROM this time on we see the rapid workings of the destiny which was finally to overtake not only the Armenians but the entire world as the result of the corrupt barbarism of Turkey and of iniquitous European diplomacy in the Near East. The appalling catastrophe which had fallen unredressed upon the little Armenian nation—such is the contagion of unrebuked evil—was but the foreshadowing of the fate which was soon to overtake the Belgians, the Serbs, the Poles, and which was to exact the heavy blood tribute of France, of the British Empire, of Italy, and even of America, and to threaten the very existence of these free and powerful states.

At the time the Western governments were thoroughly aware of their solemnly undertaken treaty obligations with regard to the Armenians, but to the worldly-wise materialists who were then shaping the fortunes of our world it seemed "safer" to ignore than to fulfil them. One wonders if even the present cataclysm has convinced statesmen of this type that there are certain crimes against humanity which mankind may not tolerate and that the violation of this moral law carries with it its own inevitable doom.

For the massacres of the Armenians did more than cry out for the decent type of statesmanship which today we recognize as imperative. They precipitated a stupendous crisis with regard to the much coveted estate of the Sick Man. The vain cry of Christian to Christian had revealed to the Sultan all too apparently the sole basis of European interest in the Near East. From henceforth he at least had nothing to fear from pseudo-Christian intervention. Hereafter, it was to be simply a pitched battle for the control of what Napoleon called the "Empire of the World," the region "which dominates the three continents upon which live ninety per cent of all mankind." And the Sultan was in a position to choose his partners. The increasingly conflicting ambitions, the moral cowardice and the venality of the Powers and his own corresponding arrogance made it only too evident that the old semi-respectable pre-massacre status could never be restored, and that the diplomacy shaped by the Great Crime might be hereafter as conscienceless as he and his chosen partners willed.

As a matter of fact it was at this very time that Germany, capitalizing every element of the situation, even the blood of the victims, openly declared herself the friend and protector of the Sultan and of the whole Islamic world, and began to lay the sure foundation of her *Drang nach Osten* scheme —her push toward world conquest. Immunity from European intervention, no matter what his crimes, and eventually a great pan-Islamic empire were the alluring enticements which she offered to the Monster of Constantinople in return for the concession to build the longed-for Bagdad Railroad, so well named the "spine of the present war." And with such designs in prospect, the blood, not only of hundreds of thousands, but of millions of innocent human beings might well be permitted to cry in vain.

We are familiar with the ghastly farce enacted by the Kaiser at Jerusalem, Damascus, and Constantinople. We see this successor to Frederick Barbarossa—that Crusader who sent the Crown to one of the princes of Lesser Armenia—paying equal homage to the tombs of Jesus, the world's Great Democrat and lover of his kind, whose "kingdom was not of this world," and to that of Saladin, the mighty Mohammedan conqueror and chief. We hear his specious words as he places a wreath upon the tomb of the "august Saracen whose sword had driven the Crusaders from Jerusalem forever."

"I seize cheerfully upon this opportunity to express my gratitude to his Imperial Majesty, the Sultan Abdul Hamid, in whose sincere love for me I glory. I assure you that the German Emperor will be the loving friend of the great Sultan Abdul Hamid, as well as of the 300,000,000 Mohammedans who, dwelling dispersed throughout the East, reverence him as their Caliph."

To cement this royal friendship, we see gifts exchanged between the two monarchs. On the one hand, all the costly Oriental carpets and other sumptuous furniture of the Palace in which the newly-made "Hadji" had been entertained; and on the other, a portrait of the German royal family, and a costly fountain donated to the Constantinople streets, still wet with the blood of 10,000 Armenian martyrs. To such base uses had a portion of Christendom become openly converted!

But this was not all. In further evidence of the infectiousness of the rampant evil of this period, it is significant to note that it was at this time that Russia, weary of having all her "legitimate" imperial designs forever thwarted, decided to emulate the West, and to throw off all pretence at protecting the Eastern Christians. Almost immediately she began to adopt something like the Turkish attitude with regard to the Armenians of the hitherto happy region of the Caucasus with a view to their ultimate annihilation. "Armenia without the Armenians," the murderous 1895 slogan of Lobanoff, the Russian minister of Foreign Affairs, indicates the trend of the new pan-Slavic policy. Russia for the Russians, Turkey for the Turks, the world for Germany!"

And thus the barbaric doctrine of Ruthlessness, fostered, we must admit, by the dishonorable compromises and moral inertia of the rest of the world, revived and spread. And for the Armenians all hope was lost except what they themselves might create and wrest from a situation which in itself was without hope. "Stranded in the East, this fragment of Europe," this sublimely picturesque defender of Christianity, this singular advocate of Democracy and Law, became at the dawn of the twentieth century, prey to a legion of enemies, more insidious and menacing than ever she had known in the whole tragic course of her tumultuous history. Never, not even in the days of Tamerlane and Genghis Khan, had she faced a situation so dire. Virtually, in the interests of the great Imperialisms, the race had been devoted to Death in the open market of the world.

Of course, the Armenians themselves were unaware of the portentous drama which was being enacted behind the scenes. They could see clearly enough that their hopes of an European intervention had been chimerical, but they could not relinquish thought of an ultimate deliverance. At any rate, the present necessity was to help themselves, and in all their history there is nothing finer or more touching than the way in which this smitten and abandoned people, rallying from its wounds and wrongs, somehow or another recovered its morale and gradually resumed its old constructive place in the general life of Turkey and of the world.

The massacres had cost the Armenians about a quarter of a million souls, and they had been followed by a new migration, necessarily limited, however, because of the Sultan's determination not to let his prey escape. Besides, there was an immense loss in wealth. Their homes had been destroyed and they had been robbed of their property. Some of the oldest business houses of Constantinople and elsewhere had been obliged to go out of business because of the impoverishment of their Armenian creditors. There was a vast stream of orphans and defenceless old people to be cared for, homes and schools and orphanages to be built, and hospitals for the sick and wounded. But this was an undertaking in which warm-hearted foreigners, and especially Americans, shared. And presently out of the wreckage came clear evidence that the aspiring spirit of the people had been by no means extinguished.

And there was need for courage and determination. For the Government had become more repressive than ever; more extortionate in its taxes, more severe in its penalties, more scandalously indifferent even to such justice as was the standard of the Turkish courts-of-law. The censorship, already excessive, became ridiculous in its watchfulness. The Kurds and Circassians were still allowed to plunder the defenceless towns and villages at will. The prisons and dungeons were filled with Armenian victims. Spies were everywhere.

To some races the alternative of submission might have suggested itself, but to the awakened Armenian spirit there appeared only the sacred necessity for further effort. Especially among the generous and enlightened youth trained in the universities of

Europe and America, the feeling arose that did the people of Europe really know the character of the sufferings, and the nature and history of the afflicted race, they would not permit their governments to remain indifferent to the pledges of elementary reform which had been made.

An energetic diplomatic propaganda was therefore begun by them in London, Paris, Tiflis, Leipzig, Geneva, Alexandria, Boston, New York, and elsewhere, with the object of "converting" Europe, and of winning the active support of America. Again, as before, the object aimed at was not separation from Turkey, but *reform*. Journals were published in English, French, and Armenian, and books and articles were written and speeches made in which the nature of the issue was elaborated upon. The Armenian leaders of the patriotic societies made overtures, too, to the Young Turks, and offered to unite with them in demanding the restoration of the constitution which Odian had drawn up and which Abdul Hamid had proclaimed and then revoked. And, in sure token of the undying spiritual vitality of the race, there sprang into passionate being a new literature, a new poetry, inspired chiefly by love of freedom and country, and more rich and powerful, more sustainedly and consciously artistic, perhaps, than any that had gone before. Aharonian, Siamento, Varoudjan, Toumanian, Tchobanian, and others—the world will some day pay its tribute to their magnificent song.[8]

The scope of this brief sketch does not permit individual tribute to the men of genius and faith who, at a period of history fundamentally hostile to the rights of small peoples, dared unreservedly to devote all their gifts and resources to the furtherance of this holy but desperate cause. But Europe—now aligned, because of German aggression in the Near East, into two definite and mutually hostile camps, each contending for the control of Turkish territory—was in no position to interest herself in the internal reforms of that country. Therefore, in spite of toil and sacrifice and the co-operation of noble individuals in England, France, America, and other countries, no definite progress was made. The appeal on behalf of Armenia became but a voice in the wilderness.

Not in all countries, however, were the efforts of the Armenian patriots equally abortive. By the opening years of the twentieth century, the struggle for national preservation in Russian Armenia had become acute, pursuant to the policy entered upon by Lobanoff at the time of the massacres. During these years the Government of the Czar attempted to bring the people into complete vassalage to a general scheme of Russification. The plan was to destroy the national identity by depriving them of their language and of their Church, and to this end the schools were closed and the property and revenues of the ancient Mother Church at Etchmiadzin were confiscated.

A singular method of terrorization was instituted by Christian Russia—one which smacks of the policy which had been entered upon so shortly before by the government of the Kaiser. The religious fanaticism of the Moslem Tartars of the Caucasian region was secretly inflamed by the local Russian officials, and they were incited to war upon their Christian neighbors, with whom they had hitherto lived in peace. As a result, the whole region was soon in the grip of a fanatical outburst. But the Armenians were well co-ordinated, and they possessed arms. Consequently they were able to defend themselves, and even to overcome the Tartar attacks. The dignified but determined passive resistance of the aged Catholicos Khrimian, too, had its effect. So the persecution fell into abeyance.

A little later, we see the untiring spirit of the Armenians again at work in the cause of human freedom, this time in Persia. All who have followed the story of Persia's ill-starred but glorious attempt to take her place among the constitutionally governed nations, are doubtless familiar with the part played by the Armenian prince, Malcolm Khan, for some years Persian minister in London, who is said "to have sowed the first seeds of constitutional government in Persia"; and with the name of the other Armenian leader, Ephrem Davidian, who later distinguished himself in the same cause. But few, I believe, are aware of the heroic career which preceded Davidian's short-lived victory for Persia, and, consequently, for his countrymen who had come under her domination. His brilliant but tragic story, so symbolic of the fortunes which have forever dogged the footsteps of his unfortunate nation, has been so admirably summarized by that remarkable woman of the same race, Mrs. Diana Agabeg Apcar, that it seems most fitting to let the tale be told in her own thrilling words.

"In 1908," she writes, "Shah Muhammad Ali Mirza was deposed and constitutional government established in Persia. The cordiality between the Armenians and the Persians was great at that period, and the leader and generalissimo of the whole successful movement was Ephrem Davidian, known in Persia as Ephrem Khan. He escaped from Saghalien prison in 1891. Fighting with a score of companions against a whole Turkish regiment in Turkish Armenia, these young men when hard pressed crossed the frontier into Russian Armenia and were there immediately seized by the Russian authorities and consigned to a prison in Saghalien. Escaping, Ephrem became the leader of the nationalistic movement in Persia in 1908, and, as is well known, not only defeated the ex-Shah's forces, but kept the peace of Teheran. Ephrem was idolized by the Persian Constitutionalists and when assassinated by the agents of the Russian government, was buried with royal honors by the Persian people."

There seems to be little need of dwelling upon the so-called revolution which at this time occurred in Turkey, and which led to the dethronement of Abdul Hamid and the proclamation of a constitution. The word "revolution" in this connection is at best a misnomer. It was an affair in which the people had absolutely no part. It was simply the seizure of power by a military clique trained in Germany or by Germans, and although it gave to the Armenians a brief period of illusory hope,[9] it does not deserve to be distinguished from the rule which preceded it, except in so far as it has proved to be more scientifically cruel and destructive.

The frightful massacre at Adana in which twenty thousand persons were slain within a few days, the very year following the proclamation, shows only too emphatically, as some one has said, that the "Young" Turks were very like the "Old." And so it came about that in a Turkey possessed of a representative parliament, the Armenians, in order to obtain security for "life, honor, and property," were once more obliged to have formal recourse to the Powers which had signed the Treaty of Berlin.

The explanation of this anomalous situation is not difficult to seek. There had been developing among the Young Turks and their followers a political credo, less ambitious, possibly, than the ancient pan-Islamic tide, but not less arrogant and ruthless; Turkey for the Turks was but a part of the pan-Turanian scheme which had come into being as a result of German stimulus and example. "In Parliament," says Viscount Bryce, "the program took such form as a bill to make the Turkish language the universal and compulsory medium of secondary education" —a death blow to Armenian progress and nationality since "the vast majority of the secondary schools of the Empire were, of course, American, Armenian or Greek." But regardless of the fact that the Turkish language was barren of a literature which would in any way meet the needs of the times, the Young Turks insisted upon this form of Ottomanization, and upon others equally impossible and reactionary. "And the Armenian deputies"—to quote Viscount Bryce again—"found themselves opposing it in concert with the liberal party, which included the Arab bloc and stood for the toleration of national individualities." In addition, the Armenians had positive demands to make, such as a mixed Gendarmarie—open to Turks and Armenians but closed to Kurds, who continued to practice their old habit of brigandage—and for an actual, and not merely nominal, equality between Christians and Moslems before the law.

But the Young Turks had become deaf to all reason. Intoxicated by the "superior race" idea, an altogether unfounded belief in their own abilities, based in part upon centuries of delusive racial privilege, had taken possession of them. And as affairs proceeded, and the actual administration of the Empire called more and more imperatively for men of practical sense and ability, it maddened them to discover that the race whom they had always despised and outlawed was really the more capable of performing the work of the state, as well as of conducting the other affairs of life.

The foundation for the jealousy which took possession of them is evident from the anaylses made by many European authorities, among them no less a personage than Dr. Paul Rohrbach, who, as an exponent of the *Drang nach Osten* program, spent four years in Turkey for the purpose of surveying the situation from every point of view. During this time he came to feel a very high and cordial admiration for the Armenians as a race, and it is evidently with a view of bringing them to the attention of the Home Government as a valuable asset in the upbuilding of the future German Eastern Empire, that he dilates upon their abilities and virtues.

According to Dr. Rohrbach (writing shortly before the outbreak of the war) the Armenians played a part in the intellectual and economic life of Turkey "entirely out of proportion to their number"; the Armenian schools supported by the voluntary offerings of the people, and exclusive of all missionary establishments, exceeded the Turkish schools four to one, and were much better; the trades and the liberal professions were in Armenian hands, and, in general, the economic life of the Empire depended upon them, and this *"not because of a singular lack of business scruple, or love of gain, but through their innate capacity for labor!"*

Dr. Rohrbach further states that their ability to read and write *Turkish,* in addition to their "general psychic energy and assiduity for labor," accounted for the relatively high number of Armenian employees in the service of the Turkish administration, without whom, he declares, "the machinery of the State would absolutely stop." And he adds that according to the testimony of the Constantinople press, the ministries of the two Armenians, Noradounghian and Haladjian—Internal Affairs and Public Works—were the only ones which had accomplished anything.

But all this was beside the purpose, so far as the "Home Government" was concerned. Probably the plan to subdue or to wreck the Armenian people had been already provisionally formulated by Constantinople and Berlin; and the two Inspectors-General commissioned in 1913 by Germany and Russia to investigate the Armenian grievances on behalf of the Signatory Powers were doubtless merely a blind, at least so far as the former was concerned. If the East was to be converted into a new type of despotism and the way made safe for a new tyranny, it was certainly not the Armenians who would play the leading and compliant part. At the suitable moment, all factors hostile to such a purpose must be eliminated, even though it meant the annihilation of an entire race.

The shadow of the ultimate catastrophe was therefore already black upon the land when Germany gave the signal for the universal conflagration.

Chapter VI

IN THE WORLD WAR

THE extreme precariousness of their position must have been sensed by the Armenians at the moment of the outbreak of the war. Through the expostulations of their representatives in the Turkish parliament and elsewhere, their grievances against the Young Turk government and their distrust of this rule had become matters of official and popular knowledge. A war would give their enemy the opportunity to wreak vengeance upon them. The military *entente* between the Young Turks and Germany was already well known and Turkish participation on the German side was more than a probability. Turkish societies, called "patriotic," had recently sent threatening letters to the Armenian Patriarch, to the editors of the Armenian newspapers, to Boghos Nubar Pasha, President of the Armenian Delegation, and to others who were helping to bring the Armenian situation before the attention of Europe. The following is one of many similar documents, signed by numbers of Turks, which these societies had sent to the Armenian press of Constantinople:

"We advise you not to speak any more of Armenian reforms. If you do the matter will become serious and we will massacre you, old and young. We will eviscerate you in the open streets, and you will find the former massacres desirable in comparison to those which we shall execute."[10]

At the same time, bands of Turkish "nationalists" had gone nightly through the streets of the Armenian quarter, marking in red and black insulting words and threats of death upon the doors of the Armenian houses, churches, and schools. Furthermore, just at this period the two Inspectors-General commissioned by the Powers to examine into the Armenian situation had already arrived!

But, aside from the actual peril of their position, there were moral reasons why the possibility of war between Turkey and the Entente should be painful and repugnant to the Armenians. By virtue of similarity of character and ideals they had always been drawn to the people of France and England, and to the people of Russia they were united not only by a certain understanding and sympathy, but, in the Caucasus, by the tie of blood. To fight Russia would be to help in the slaughter of their own brothers. Hitherto, in all the Turco-European wars except the Balkan War of 1912, in which as citizens of constitutionally governed Turkey they had been obliged to participate, they had been spared the necessity of taking the field on the side of their deadly enemy because of their proscription as Christians from the Turkish military service. But now, if the constitution were lived up to, they would, in the event of war, be obliged to take up arms in defence of the despotic Young Turks and the Central Powers, and on behalf of principles which they had always abhorred. What had they been consistently throughout their history but a lance never in rest, a pilgrim always on the road, a martyr forever at the stake in the cause of political and religious democracy? A sardonic reminder of their known allegiance to these things appeared in the Constantinople comic paper, "Karagöz" in the early days of the war.[11] It depicted two Turks in earnest discussion. "Where do you get your war news?" asked one. "I do not need war news," replied the other. "I can follow the faces of the Armenians I meet. When they are happy I know the Allies are winning, and when they are depressed I know that the Germans have had a victory."

Just as there is no equivalent for the word "compromise" in all their rich language, so there had been no room for it in the course of their hazardous national existence. It was too late for them to adopt a renegade policy. At best the officials and the men of military age could but perform their duties grimly and without show of enthusiasm, hoping against hope that they might thereby purchase immunity for the civilian population from the Djihad, or the massacre, which a general disturbance in Turkey was likely to portend, and of which there were already threatening rumors.

As Turkish sympathy for the Central Powers grew more and more apparent, it became the one aim of the Armenian leaders to dissuade the Government from joining forces with these nations. As members of the Turkish parliament and as Ottoman citizens they tried to make it clear that such a course would be fatal to the life of the Empire. In this opinion some of the Turks of the Conservative party are said to have concurred. But when the Young Turks showed no inclination to heed the advice, some of the deputies of the interior provinces and other Armenian leaders decided to meet in conference at Van and Erzeroum for the purpose of determining what course, in the event of war, would best safeguard the Armenian population.

It is vitally important for us to realize that the question of winning the Armenians to the side of the Central Powers had already been uppermost in the minds of the Young Turks; and that at a time when so much hinged upon the attitude which this or that people would take, when other nationalities were bargaining back and forth for terms with both of the great contestants, the Armenians of Turkey, too, had at least an ostensible chance to barter their honor for their lives. There is every reason to believe that their ultimate destruction had been determined upon from the outset. (See "Documents presented to Viscount Grey" by Viscount Bryce—English Blue Book.) But the Young Turks, intriguers as well as murderers, preferred, if possible, first to utilize their prey for their own disgraceful ends. The story of this attempt and its failure of accomplishment reflects the sheer heroism of the Armenian people and is one of the noblest episodes in the annals of the war.

The scene occurred simultaneously in the cities already referred to, Van and Erzeroum, —Van, originally founded by Semiramis as a summer city, later the capital of a long line of Armenian kings; a city overlooking the great salt lake of Van, five thousand feet above sea level; a beautiful city made more beautiful by the industry of her inhabitants; a city of orchards, vineyards, and gardens; and Erzeroum, situated at an even higher altitude and, like Van, in the center of that part of ancient Armenia to the soil of which the race had clung with the greatest tenacity.

It was to these classic Armenian strongholds that the Enver-Talaat government sent their representatives for the purpose of inducing the Armenian leaders, assembled there in convention, to incite their brethren across the Russian frontier to take up arms on the side of Turkey.

The story comes to us through many channels, but I quote it as given in Document 21 in the English Blue Book already referred to:

> According to the project of the Young Turks, the Armenians were to pledge themselves to form legions of volunteers and to send them to the Caucasus with the Turkish propagandists, to prepare the way there for the insurrection.
>
> The Young Turk representatives had already brought their propagandists with them to Erzeroum—27 individuals of Persian, Turkish, Lesghian and Circassian nationality. The Turks tried to persuade the Armenians that a Caucasian insurrection was inevitable; that very shortly the Tartars, Georgians and mountaineers would revolt, and that the Armenians would consequently be obliged to follow them.
>
> They even sketched the future map of the Caucasus.
>
> The Turks offered to the Georgians the provinces of Koutais, and of Tiflis, the Batoum district and a part of the province of Trebizond; to the Tartars, Shousha, the mountain country as far as Vladivkavkaz, Bakou,

and a part of the province of Elisavetpol; to the Armenians they offered Kars, the province of Erivan, a part of Elisavetpol, a fragment of the province of Erzeroum, Van and Bitlis. According to the Young Turk scheme, all these groups were to become autonomous under a Turkish protectorate. The Erzeroum Congress refused these proposals, and advised the Young Turks not to hurl themselves into the European conflagration.

The Young Turks were irritated by this advice.

"This is treason!" cried Boukhar-ed-Din-Shakir, one of the delegates from Constantinople: "You take sides with Russia in a moment as critical as this; you refuse to defend the Government; you forget that you are enjoying its hospitality!"

But the Armenians held to their decision.

Once more before the outbreak of war between Russia and Turkey, the Young Turks tried to obtain the Armenians' support. This time they opened their *pourparlers* with more moderate proposals, and negotiated with the Armenian representatives of each Vilayet. At Van, the *pourparlers* were conducted by the provincial governor Tahsin Bey, and by Nadji Bey; at Moush, by Servet Bey and Iskhan Bey; at Erzeroum by the same Tahsin Bey and by others.

The project of an Armenian rising in the Caucasus was abandoned. Instead, the Ottoman Armenians were to unite themselves with the Transcaucasian Tartars, whose insurrection was, according to the Young Turks, a certainty.

Once more the Armenians refused.

From the moment the war broke out, the Armenian soldiers had presented themselves for service at their regimental depots, but they refused categorically to form irregular bands.

In case of war between Turkey and Russia, they said, the Armenians on both sides of the frontier must do their duty by their respective governments.

Meanwhile another sinister drama was being enacted on the other side of the Russian frontier. When Russia learned that the Turks were mobilizing, she sent representatives to address the Armenians of the Caucasus and to promise them that if they would help her to the utmost she would guarantee future autonomy to the Armenians of Turkey. Word, too, is said to have come to them— unofficially, I believe,—from the other Powers of the Entente telling them that if they would do all in their power to hold the Turk at bay on the Eastern front all help would be forthcoming from France and England. The race in whose defence not one single shot had ever been fired had suddenly become, because of their strategic position, a determining factor in that critical region—one of the gateways to India. And they were being leaned upon by a world which had abandoned them in their long struggle!

The Armenians of the Caucasus knew very well that the designs of Russia were fundamentally unfriendly to them, but they recognized the world aspect of the struggle, and readily agreed to organize volunteer corps to help the regular army, and a committee was formed at Tiflis to recruit them. But the Armenian regular soldiers, to the number of 160,000, and the 20,000 volunteers who almost immediately responded to the call, showed such eagerness for action that Russia became alarmed. A brilliant Armenian defence on the home soil might lead to national ambition and future complications. So, to the consternation of the Armenian community, most of the regulars were transferred to the Poland and Galician fronts, and old Russian reservists who knew nothing of this tangled mountain region were sent to guard the lines. Moreover, Russia equipped but grudgingly the Armenian volunteers and instead of sending them as a compact unit, arranged to have them scattered over the front.

The Armenians saw that Russia was not really with them. The High Command not only did all in its power to make the situation difficult for the soldiers: it behaved in a very unkind and unscrupulous way to the Armenian civilian population. Still the Armenians tried to keep their spirits. The volunteers were popular with the Russian rank and file and, eager to have part in a war waged against their most cruel foe, they overlooked the unsatisfactory stand of the Russian government.

While these events were progressing in Russia, the Young Turks, infuriated by the refusal of the Armenians of Turkey to acquiesce in their nefarious and much counted-upon Caucasian scheme, were putting the loyalty of these their fellow citizens to the severest tests by "requisitioning" their property in a wholly wanton and ominous way, and by sending battalions formed exclusively of Armenians to the most exposed fronts, there to be mown down by French and British shells. Naturally these outrages filled the Armenians with intense indignation, but in general they restrained themselves, and carefully refrained from any act of even seeming disloyalty, in order to give no pretext for further reprisals.

But there was no avoiding the end that had been prepared for them. It had been too long an obsession of the Turkish mind. And now that it was clear both to the Turks and to their German accomplices that the Armenians would never consent to become the tools of Turco-German design, there was every reason, to their mind, why it should be immediately accomplished. For the first time in years they felt themselves wholly free of the restraint which the attitude of Europe had hitherto to some extent imposed upon them. More than that, they enjoyed the full protection of a Power whose philosophy coincided exactly with their own and whom they believed to be invincible. The war hung like a curtain of fire between them and the outside world. In the chaos of the moment they could work out their intentions wholly unchecked and without fear of punishment.

But unlike the days of Abdul Hamid, some of the Armenians were now armed, and unless they could be rendered defenceless the struggle would take on the character not of massacre but of civil war, an eventuality by all means to be avoided.

As a preliminary step, therefore, they decided to murder the Armenian soldiery throughout the country simultaneously and *en masse,* after forming them into "labor battalions"; and at the same time to decoy and murder the prominent Armenian leaders. Then they would fall on the civilian population, and as Talaat Bey expressed it, "put an end to the Armenian question for the next fifty years." It was a piece of perfectly regular Turco-Prussian strategy.

In less than a year the deed has been accomplished. The Armenians of Turkey to the number of about a million, old and young, rich and poor, and of both sexes, had been collectively drowned, burned, bayonetted, starved, bastinadoed, or otherwise tortured to death, or else deported on foot, penniless, and without food, to the burning Arabian deserts.

How shall we name the dastardly crime which robbed them of life and homeland? How shall we describe that catastrophe, the detailed accounts of which, as Mr. A. P. Hacobian, of London, in his book "Armenia and the War," so fitly says, "unfolds to the horrified gaze of mankind a vast column of human smoke and anguish rising to the heavens as the incense of the most fearful yet most glorious mass-martyrdom the world has ever seen"? To attempt to do so—is it not almost an irreverence to the august dead? We of the powerful West, who might long ago have averted all this agony and appalling waste of precious human resource, had we been honorable enough to fulfill even the most elementary obligations of our great religion—what is there for us to say by way of sympathetic tribute in the presence of this sublime agony, this breaking of a nation's body, this rending of a nation's soul?

It is for us to remember that they went to their death, man, woman, and child, not only as martyrs to the sacred ideal for which their fathers had made immemorial sacrifices; not only as victims of hideous despotism and base political intrigue; but also virtually as noble prisoners of war in the interest of our cause which, in spite of threatening pressure, they had resolutely refused to betray. A poignantly magnanimous climax to a singularly unbefriended national career! Yet, although until "the future dares forget the Past, their fate and fame shall be an echo and a light unto eternity," how would the great heart of mankind wish that in the midst of the flames which were destroying our temporizing and materialistic civilization, these, the wholly innocent, might somehow have been spared!

But, no, amid the smoke and glare of the universal conflagration, the tragedy plunges forward, and a scene from which we shrink forces itself upon our eyes. Those cordons of men and boys bound together and hurled from precipices or thrown into the sea, or bayonetted, still warm and sometimes still breathing, into great trench graves which they themselves had dug, or felled by the axe, each in his turn, as they wait, herded in lonely valley, or in prison yard, or rained upon by the fire of great guns as they stand awaiting "orders," or listening to the reading of some spurious proclamation; those women "praying in the flames," or lying in their own and their children's blood upon the hearthstones or by the roadside; the unending procession of the deported who, uprooted from their ancestral home, dragged from the beautiful springtime of the Armenian highlands, are driven forth to the scorching deserts, there to die of hunger, heat and drought; the mothers dying in childbirth upon the road, or begging the casual passer-by to take from them their adored and lovely babies and being refused even that tragic boon; those mothers who, unable to carry their children, or to endure the sight of their suffering, await with both eagerness and dread the sight of lake or river into which they may cast them as a final act of mercy; those children crying for their murdered parents, for their lost brothers and sisters, as they too march forward to their own deaths; the maidens weeping for their lost lovers or struggling with the demons who drag them off to slavery; all while Turkish and German officers look brutally on, and give orders to the convicts—recruited from the prisons for this murderous purpose—who herd the procession ever forward beneath the blows of their heavy goads: these are but the blurred outlines of that immense hecatomb to the gods of Lust and Blood which dominated the land.

But the dead will not permit us to remain with them. There are other heroes who command our homage. In the midst of the universal carnage, the civilian population of certain towns and villages, raised to a pitch of superhuman courage by the knowledge of what threatened both them and their nation, waged a defensive warfare which, considering all the circumstances, may justly be regarded as absolutely unmatched. In most cases, after these stubborn resistances had failed for want of ammunition, the inhabitants were burned in their churches, or in wooden concentration camps erected for the purpose, put to the sword or tortured to death; but in the districts bordering the Russian frontier they sometimes managed to escape by throwing in their lot with the Russo-Armenian volunteers and the regular Russian army, retreating or advancing with these as Fortune dictated.

These defenses, although part of the chain which united those of Belgium, France, Italy, and Serbia, were conducted under circumstances which recall Thermopylæ, and the famous sieges of antiquity. They are destined to live forever in the immortal Hero-Book of our battle-scarred world. In the midst of a struggle carried on by means of submarines, gas bombs, air ships and tanks, these pictures of primitive warfare flash out upon us veritably as from the Classic Age.

Although the records of the towns and villages of each vilayet shine with deeds of individual and community valor, in certain spots, like Van, Sassoun, and Djibal-Moussa, Armenian heroism was illustrated in more commanding if not in more intensified form.

The wonderful story of Djibal-Moussa, a town of Cilician Armenia overlooking the Mediterranean, is bound to become a classic, both because of its gallant and picturesque quality, and because of the thrilling rescue of the beleagured mountaineers by the God-sent French flagship, *Ste. Jeanne d'Arc!*

The resistance of Sassoun, too, although fatal in its ending, will forever enhearten the souls of valiant men. Let me quote the story as it comes to us in Document 22 of the English Blue Book:

While the "Butcher" battalions of Djevdet Bey and the regulars of Kiazim Bey were engaged in Bitlis and Moush, some cavalry were sent to Sassoun early in July to encourage the Kurds who had been defeated by the Armenians at the beginning of June. The Turkish cavalry invaded the lower valley of Sassoun and captured a few villages after stout fighting. In the meantime the reorganized Kurdish tribes attempted to close on Sassoun from the South, West, and North. During the last fortnight of July almost incessant fighting went on, sometimes even during the night. On the whole, the Armenians held their own on all fronts and expelled the Kurds from their advanced positions. However, the people of Sassoun had other anxieties to worry about. The population had doubled since their brothers who had escaped from the plains had sought refuge in their mountains; the millet crop of the last season had been a failure; all honey, fruit, and other local produce had been consumed, and the people had been feeding on unsalted roast mutton (they had not even any salt to make the mutton more sustaining); finally, the ammunition was in no way sufficient for the requirements of heavy fighting. But the worst had yet to come. Kiazim Bey, after reducing the town and the plain of Moush, rushed his army to Sassoun for a new effort to overwhelm these brave mountaineers. Fighting was renewed on all fronts throughout the Sassoun district. Big guns made carnage among the Armenian ranks. Roupen tells me that Gorioun, Dikran, and twenty others of their best fighters were killed by a single shell, which burst in their midst. Encouraged by the presence of guns, the cavalry and Kurds pushed on with relentless energy.

The Armenians were compelled to abandon the outlying lines of their defence and were retreating day by day into the heights of Antok, the central block of the mountains, some 10,000 feet high. The non-combatant women and children and their large flocks of cattle greatly hampered the free movements of the defenders, whose number had already been reduced from 3,000 to about half that figure. Terrible confusion prevailed during the Turkish attacks as well as the Armenian counter attacks. Many of the Armenians smashed their rifles after firing the last cartridge and grasped their revolvers and daggers. The Turkish regulars and Kurds, amounting now to something like 30,000 altogether, pushed higher and higher up the heights and surrounded the main Armenian position at close quarters. Then followed one of those desperate and heroic struggles for life which have always been the pride of mountaineers. Men, women, and children fought with knives, scythes, stones, and anything else they could handle. They rolled blocks of stone down the steep slopes, killing many of the enemy. In a frightful hand-to-hand combat, women were seen thrusting their knives into the throats of Turks and thus accounting for many of them. On the 5th of August, the last day of the fighting, the bloodstained rocks of Antok were captured by the Turks. The Armenian warriors of Sassoun, except those who had worked round to the rear of the Turks to attack them on their flanks, had died in battle."

There is a wealth of material concerning Van, which the Armenians held for four weeks against a German-led Turkish army. To defend themselves, the civilians were obliged to manufacture their own powder, to construct their own mortars, and even to make their own guns. We learn that they succeeded in making from two to four thousand cartridges a day, that "the blacksmiths made spears to be used if necessary when the ammunition was all gone"; that they dug trenches and underground passages through which they blew up Turkish barracks and entrenchments; and that in the very midst of the most furious bombardments, the Normal School band played Armenian national airs and the *Marseillaise* to enhearten the fighters!

"All the people of Van, without exception," says an eye-witness, "worked with one soul. Those who had arms and were able to fight rushed to take their stand and stop the Turks from entering the Armenian quarters, and those who were able to work took spade and shovel to go to strengthen the fighting men's positions by constructing trenches and walls. The little boys worked as scouts, the women and girls undertook the care of the sick and of the children and did all the cooking and sewing for the fighters.

"To save their lives and honor all the Armenians of Van had placed their services at the disposal of the Military Council, who awarded crosses and medals to encourage those who were worthy of them. I was present when a little girl received one of these medals. During the retaking of a position in Angous Tzor she bravely went ahead, spied out the ground and brought back news that the Turks had laid no traps for the advancing Armenian soldiers."

The actual fighting force of Van numbered only 1500 men, but by their skill and strategy, no less than by their valor, and with the devoted backing of the other inhabitants, they forced the enemy finally to evacuate their positions. "At midnight, on the 17th of May, 1915," says the same eye-witness, "the town criers went through the town crying 'Victory.'

... The whole city was in an uproar; some went to look at the entrenchments: others to look at the burned Turkish quarters; and others to visit the fortress, captured that night, and over which a banner waved, bearing the symbol of the Cross.

"Shortly after, news came that the Russian army with the Armenian Volunteers was in sight. The joy of the people was boundless; tears of gladness and of emotion for what they had suffered during the past month rolled down their cheeks as they made them welcome." They fired salvos from the captured Turkish guns and "laid the keys of the captured city and Castle at the feet of the Russian General."

But to the eternal infamy of the Czar's government, the heroic resistance of the Van and other Armenians of the region, as well as the valiant efforts of the Russo-Armenian volunteers, was partially undone by the mysterious conduct of the Russian army. The prospect of an eventual occupation by Russia of the Armenian plateau, as arranged by a secret treaty between her and the other Powers of the Entente—later published by the Bolsheviki—was evidently dictating a policy hostile to them. An unaccountable retreat was almost immediately ordered, which exposed the now defenseless population either to all the ravages of a forced march over the frontier or to the mercy of the oncoming Turks. The obvious design was to accomplish the depopulation of the country, and thus to prepare the way for the Russian colonization, which even now was beginning to take form in the bands of Russian Cossack peasants who were actually pre-empting Armenian lands.[12]

This shameless and terrible policy was crushing to the spirits of the Armenians of Russia, as well as to the already agonized hearts of those still on Turkish soil. But surrender was impossible, and they persisted in their desperate struggle against the Turco-German program. The fall of the Czar's government, which in the natural order of things would have been to them a blessing, only aggravated and intensified their immediate peril. They had been deprived of the bulk of their own fighting men at the beginning of the war, it will be remembered, by transfer to the Western front, and when the Russian regulars were withdrawn, they were thrown entirely upon their own meager resources. The only recourse was to organize what resistance they could, in conjunction with the Georgians.

So early as May, 1917, anticipating this general demoralization of the Russian army, the Armenians had sent representatives to Petrograd to urge upon the Kerensky government the speedy return of the Armenian regulars for the defense of the Caucasian front. But the government could do little for them. The delegates therefore formed in Petrograd a committee of Armenian military men for the purpose of finding ways and means of effecting this end. With all their efforts, however, they succeeded, in six months, in transferring only 35,000 men. These were joined with volunteers and formed into army corps.

To add to the terrors of the situation, the Tartars rose in open league with the Turks and were burning bridges, cutting railroad communications, and attacking the Armenians from all sides. This was an enormous handicap, but the Armenians none the less succeeded in fighting their way through and holding the front against the advancing Turkish army.

Then came the Brest-Litovsk Treaty, by the stipulations of which part of Russian Armenia was ceded to the Turks! This the Armenians had the daring utterly to repudiate, and for a time, with the co-operation of the Georgians, they continued to resist the Turkish assault. Then the Georgians capitulated, and the Armenians went on with the struggle single-handed, conducting themselves so valiantly that as late as July 14, 1918, Mr. Balfour was able to say in the British Parliament: "We follow with the deepest sympathy and admiration the brave resistance which the Armenians are offering to the Turkish army." And although the Armenians of the Erivan district were, in the language of Lord Robert Cecil of the British Foreign Office, "at length compelled by main force to suspend hostilities" and come to terms with the foe, other Armenians of the Caucasus, under the leadership of Generals

Andranik, Nazarbekof, Pakradooni, and Rostome, are continuing the fight to the present hour.

And of the Armenians of Erivan, Lord Robert says: "Great Britain and her allies understand the cruel necessity which forced them to take that step, and look forward to the time, perhaps not far distant, when the allied victories may reverse their undeserved misfortunes"; and he acknowledges their services at length, saying, among other things, *"that they had thrown themselves into the breach which the Russian breakdown left open in Asia by taking over the Caucasian front, and for five months delaying the Turks' advance,—and that they thus rendered important service to the British army in Mesopotamia."*

While these sublime actors were playing this immensely significant part, unsustained by the help or fellowship of their European comrades at arms, and scarcely knowing what the Fates, even in the event of victory, would have in store for them, but resting ever on their abiding faith in Ultimate Justice, other Armenians, of the Dispersion, were fighting with the Allied forces in the Foreign Legion of France, with the English in Palestine and Mesopotamia, and in the United States army. And the civilian Armenians, men and women, were doing all in their power, as doctors, nurses, engineers, Red Cross, and Liberty Loan workers, to help on the general cause of human freedom. The welcome and encouragement which these received from the Allied governments brought new life to their lacerated but undying hope of an emancipated Armenia—a hope which became assurance when America, taking the sword, announced for all mankind the new international Apocalypse:

"BUT THE RIGHT IS MORE PRECIOUS THAN PEACE, AND WE SHALL FIGHT FOR THE THINGS WHICH WE HAVE ALWAYS CARRIED NEAREST OUR HEARTS—FOR DEMOCRACY, FOR THE RIGHT OF THOSE WHO SUBMIT TO AUTHORITY TO HAVE A VOICE IN THEIR OWN GOVERNMENT, FOR THE RIGHTS AND LIBERTIES OF SMALL NATIONS, FOR A UNIVERSAL DOMINION OF RIGHT BY SUCH A CONCERT OF FREE PEOPLES AS SHALL BRING PEACE AND SAFETY TO ALL NATIONS AND MAKE THE WORLD ITSELF AT LAST FREE."

Chapter VII

IN THE WORLD COURT

"WHEN Tamerlane arrived before Sivas," we are told, "the pearl of Armenia, thousands of children met him with garlands of roses. He had both the children and the roses crushed under the hoofs of his horses." And on the neighboring plain, —called to this day "The Black Field,"—he erected one of his huge pyramids of skulls. This was in the fourteenth century.

In 1915, the descendants of Tamerlane, in union with the Government of Germany, were responsible for crimes throughout the length and breadth of the Turkish Empire, before the magnitude, the cruel finesse, the "cold commanded lust" of which even the horrors of their ancient prototype pale. Of this the testimony of Signor Gorrini, Italian Consul-General at Trebizond, published in the journal "Il Messaggero" of Rome, August 25, 1915, and republished in the English Blue Book,

concerning the fate of the Armenians of
Trebizond alone would serve as ample proof:[13]

"It was a real extermination and slaughter of the
innocents," he says, "an unheard-of thing, a black page
stained with the flagrant violation of the most sacred
rights of humanity, of Christianity, of nationality.
The Armenian Catholics, too, who in the past had
always been respected and excepted from the massacres
and persecutions, were this time treated worse than
any—again by the orders of the Central Government.
There were about 14,000 Armenians at Trebizond—
Gregorians, Catholics, and Protestants. They had
never caused disorders or given occasion for collective
measures of police. When I left Trebizond, not a
hundred of them remained.

"From the 24th of June, the date of the publication
of the infamous decree, until the 23rd of July, the date
of my own departure from Trebizond, I no longer slept
or ate; I was given over to nerves and nausea, so
terrible was the torment of having to look on at the
wholesale execution of these defenceless, innocent
creatures.

"The passing of the gangs of Armenian exiles beneath
the windows and before the door of the Consulate; their
prayers for help, when neither I nor any other could
do anything to answer them; the city in a state of siege,
guarded at every point by 15,000 troops in complete war
equipment, by thousands of police agents, by bands of
volunteers and by the members of the 'Committee of

Union and Progress'; the lamentations, the tears, the abandonments, the imprecations, the many suicides, the instantaneous deaths from sheer terror, the sudden unhinging of men's reason, the conflagrations, the shooting of victims in the city, the ruthless searches through the houses and in the countryside; the hundreds of corpses found every day along the exile road; the young women converted by force to Islam or exiled like the rest; the children torn away from their families or from the Christian schools, and handed over by force to Moslem families, or else placed by hundreds on board ship in nothing but their shirts, and then capsized and drowned in the Black Sea and the River Deyirmen Deré —these are my last ineffaceable memories of Trebizond, memories which still, at a month's distance, torment my soul and almost drive me frantic. When one has had to look on for a whole month at such horrors, at such protracted tortures, with absolutely no power of acting as one longed to act, the question naturally and spontaneously suggests itself, whether all the cannibals and all the wild beasts in the world have not left their hiding places and retreats, left the virgin forests of Africa, Asia, America, and Oceanica, to make their rendezvous at Stamboul. I should prefer to close our interview at this point, with the solemn asseveration that this black page in Turkey's history calls for the most uncompromising reproach and for the vengeance of all Christendom. If they knew all the things that I know, all that I have had to see with my eyes and hear with my ears, all Christian powers that are still neutral would be impelled to rise up against Turkey and cry anathema against her inhuman Government and her ferocious 'Committee of Union and Progress,' and they would extend the responsibility to Turkey's Allies, who tolerate or even shield with their strong arm these execrable crimes, which have not their equal in history, either modern or ancient. Shame, horror and disgrace!"

For almost six centuries Armenia has been compelled to sacrifice her children and her roses—her flesh and blood, her culture, and the fruits of her toil—to an insatiable Moloch of savagery and greed, and to the later years of this ordeal by blood and fire the great outside world has remained, we must repeat, a passive spectator. One of these mass-sacrifices was exacted, as we know, so short a time before the war as the year 1909, when 20,000 persons were massacred at Adana and in its environs. But not a movement was made to arrest the holocaust. Other gods, in addition to those of Turkey, required then their blood oblations. Now, however, the vengeance which follows violated moral law has finally overtaken all the world and, in the vision born of agony and remorse, the world will now make to Armenia what amends it can.

And what are these amends? In a word, they are the restoration to the Armenian people of their ancient fatherland where, in the free exercise of their genius and devotion, they may have the opportunity of building a state which shall be worthy of the sacrifices they have immemorially made for the sake of religion, nationality, progress and freedom. We cannot give them back their dead. But we can and must make this belated act of reparation. It is America's and the Allies' sacred promise that justice shall at length be done to the small nationalities. And to what people does the world owe more than to this, which veritably has been sacrificed for the sins of the world?

The solution commends itself even on other grounds than the all-sufficing one of justice. If not to the Armenians, to whom should we grant their ancient patrimony? What other race installed in this region, on the borderland of East and West, would serve world needs so well as they,—they who have been repeatedly called the "natural intermediaries between Orient and Occident"; they whose administrative ability has already been so amply demonstrated in the number of statesmen they have given to the world, and whose industrial and commercial abilities, whose sobriety and perseverance, are matters of common knowledge. Even in modern days, have they not filled high administrative posts in the service of the British Empire, of Russia, Turkey, and Persia? It is acknowledged that England's success in governing Egypt is largely traceable to the genius of Nubar Pasha who, both because of his personal gifts and his Armenian origin, was able sympathetically to interpret the needs of both East and West, and to whom, upon his death, the Mohammedans and Christians of Egypt united to erect a monument. As ministers of public instruction, as prime ministers, as ambassadors and as all kinds of lesser officials, they have figured successfully in the political life of all these countries. And as for the question of national defence, what race is better able to defend order than this which has proved itself the bravest of the brave and which, under Russia, has never been without

its distinguished warriors, from the days of
the general, Prince Pagratian, who was "the
opponent of Napoleon in 1812," down to
those of General Samsonoff who died on the
Poland front in the present war "trying to
relieve the strain on Paris," and General
Andranik and his colleagues, last in the
defence of the Caucasian front. The fact
that the Turks, by resorting to the device
of keeping them unarmed throughout the
centuries, were able to murder them at will
is merely a proof of Turkish cowardice.
Whenever they were known to possess arms
they were generally avoided by both Turks
and Kurds. In the Caucasus, Russia has
depended very largely upon them in the maintenance of order. It was they who constituted, to a great extent, the gendarmerie.

Moreover, if not in a free Armenia, where
then shall we place this race? It is not to be
thought for a moment that we shall expect
them to live again under some Turkish
hegemony. To expect them to submit to the
authority of the would-be annihilators of their
nation would be to do a fundamental violence
to the moral nature of all mankind. It would

signify a return to that hideous pre-war morality, in which fair was so often foul and foul was so often fair. Even before the conclusion of hostilities the world has fully made up its mind upon this point. The merits and claims both of the Armenians and of the Turks it has already clearly defined. The verdict of Mr. William T. Stead that the Turk is but "a barbarian encamped upon the ashes of the civilizations which he destroyed," is only one echo from the chorus of classic and contemporary British and Latin opinion, while Heinrich von Treitschke's view may suggest even to defeated Germany the undesirability of further alliance with, or support of, this monstrous and anachronistic rule. "A near future," he writes, "will, it is to be hoped, blot out the scandal that such heathendom should ever have established itself on European soil. What has this Turkish Empire done in three entire centuries? It has done nothing but destroy."

For an American judgment with regard to Turkey's past and future, we may turn to the words of Mr. Henry Morgenthau, recent American ambassador to Constantinople, who was witness to the evil power of the Turk as it displayed itself in the terrible year of 1915.

"After 450 years of misrule," Mr. Morgenthau says, "the Turks at last are going to be deprived of their domination over the Christian, Jewish, and Arabian population of Turkey. There must be no maudlin sentiment or emotional sympathy about their treatment. They stand convicted of wholesale murder in the first degree, of committing the most atrocious crimes and beastly tortures of the ages; of maintaining an unjust and incompetent government.

"They have demonstrated their absolute inability to govern either themselves or the nations that they have conquered.

"They have never assimilated the peoples whose territory they have overrun.

"They have lived all these years as parasites, maintaining their power by brute strength.

"They have really given nothing to these countries, no architecture, no literature, no art, no progress of any kind.

"They have sapped the life-blood and the energy of the occupants of these lands.

"They have deprived the people of security of life and property, thereby taking away all incentives to any unusual energy or to the keeping in line with the progress of the time.

"In fact they have cowed the people into a condition of rebellious though subdued submission. They have ruled by might and fear and not by right and love. . . . They have deprived themselves of the best part of their population. They have robbed, pillaged and murdered as only the most conscienceless brood of barbarians could do."

On the other hand there is the record of Armenia, a record, in the words of the French writer, M. Emile Pignot, of "an entire people bruised by the heaviest chains, lacerated by the most oppressive yoke, yet standing unbowed in the face of all sufferings, of all tyrannies, of all betrayal, of all infamies, erect upon all the Golgothas of torture, and proclaiming to the world the invincibility of its soul,"—a race whose "leaders have fallen in order that from their closed eyes might shine more clearly, more luminously, and more imperishably, the light of their national genius"; a race described by M. Deschanel,

President of the Chamber of Deputies and Member of the Academy, as having been able "even in the shadow of its slavery," to guard "the secret spring of letters, of the arts, and of liberty of conscience"; a race characterized by the Honorable Andrew D. White, former Ambassador to Germany and President of Cornell University, as "one of the finest races in the world, physically, morally and intellectually"; by Viscount Bryce as "of conspicuous brain power, with a capacity for intellectual and moral progress, as well as with a natural tenacity of will and purpose, beyond that of all their neighbors"; and by Dr. James L. Barton, Secretary of the American Board of Foreign Missions and for eight years President of Euphrates College, as "religious, industrious and faithful, . . . not inferior in mental ability to any race on earth."

If the future of Armenia were sure to be settled solely upon the shining merit of the Armenian cause, or by the universally approving testimony of the eminent men and women of all races who have loved and defended it, this little nation would scarcely need to present its claims before the World Court. But in that case neither would justice have been so long, so disgracefully, and so disastrously delayed. Both the history of the Near East and the fact of the present war which has ensued in large degree as a consequence of this question, have revealed to us the depths to which men are capable of descending in the scramble for territory and power; and they suggest the necessity of our being upon our guard against the apologists for evil who, in one form or another, are certain to make themselves heard at the final settlement.

With regard to the dangers inherent in the Turkish situation it may not be amiss to quote a statement made by Mr. Samuel S. McClure in his *Obstacles to Peace;* "However difficult the various questions involved in the peace settlement," he writes,—"and no one can exaggerate the almost insoluble questions—the real problem of the war is Asiatic Turkey. The settlement of this question may involve a continuous series of devastating wars at longer or shorter intervals for generations."

This was written in 1916, when the world situation wore a different aspect from that of today. The Russian Revolution had not then occurred and America had not entered the war, and there was no reason to suppose that the partition of Turkey, along traditional lines, among the victorious European powers would not follow the cessation of hostilities. But even today in a world made new by these events, Mr. McClure's statement still stands in the opinion of all who are giving thought to the issues of that decisive battle of the World War which we are in the habit of naming the Peace Congress. The Turkish Empire still presents possibilities for rivalry and discord which are not common to the other countries the destinies of which are now a matter of world debate. Mr. McClure's words are more than a statement of generally recognized truth. They are a solemn warning. They suggest the imperative necessity for a determined pre-Peace Congress educational propaganda which shall eliminate the possibility of any such settlement as might lead to future disaster.

We are all fully aware of the extent to which Turkey, both because of her criminal character and her central geographical position, has already figured not only in this but in numbers of other wars which have embroiled Europe. Should she again be the occasion or the means of precipitating another general war, it would probably mean the destruction of Western civilization, for, as the great historian Ferrera has recently said, we could not survive another such catastrophe. To attempt to solve this outstanding problem upon the old lines of expediency and compromise would be to point the sword at the very heart of Europe and America.

The drama which I have attempted swiftly to trace in the foregoing sketch is destined therefore to have a tremendous epilogue, since upon the solution of this central problem may be said to depend the fate not only of our chief protagonists but of the entire world. Hence this people become once more the moral arbiters, as it were, of a universal destiny; the token by which shall be registered the triumph either of Democracy or Autocracy, our victory or our defeat.

In the imperial and economic point of view of the baser elements of Europe as well as in that of the Turkish despotism, the region so recently contested for will still be an object of extreme covetousness. And by evidence already at hand we may anticipate the battle which these factors will wage on their own behalf. Claims will be put forward both in the interests of the present ruling race and of the foreign imperialists and exploiters; and in case it seems better to serve these designs, Turkey may be cited as calling for quite another solution from that which should be applied to other disintegrating empires— Russia or Austria for example; and Turkey-in-Europe, as requiring settlement by a code different from that demanded by conditions in Turkey-in-Asia. We are concerned only with the solution based upon the grounds of absolute justice which alone, we hope, the peoples of the world will tolerate. And for guidance we can do no better than to turn to Gladstone, that prophet of the Near Eastern question whose noble and inspired warnings Europe ignored, to humanity's inestimable cost. Mr. Gladstone is discussing this same issue as it presented itself following the Treaty of Berlin:

"My meaning, Sir," he says, "was that,

for one, I utterly repelled the doctrine that the power of Turkey is to be dragged to the ground for the purpose of handing over the Dominion that Turkey now exercises to some other great State, be that State either Russia or Austria or even England. In my opinion such a view is utterly false, and even ruinous, and has been the source of the main difficulties in which the Government have been involved, and in which they have involved the country. I hold that those provinces of the Turkish Empire, which have been so cruelly and unjustly ruled, ought to be regarded as existing, not for the sake of any other Power whatever but for the sake of the populations by whom they are inhabited. The object of our desire ought to be the development of those populations on their own soil, as its proper masters, and as the persons with a view to whose welfare its destination ought to be determined."

This point of view is, of course, none other than the one to which both the Allies and America have solemnly committed themselves. It is simply another lamp, a glorious one from the Past, to show the way. If this majestic estate called the Turkish Empire is to be rescued permanently from the despoiler and the conquest seeker, it will be because a settlement has been found adapted to the just and legitimate interests of all the *native populations,* Armenian, Syrian, Greek, Arab, Jew, and even Turk. What form this general and complicated settlement may take is not here a matter under speculation. But the solution called for by the Armenian claims is fortunately not so indefinite or so involved as to prohibit prophecy. While it may be true that, as Mr. Arnold Toynbee has said, the frontiers of the future Armenian state "cannot be forecast, they must include the Six Vilayets —so often promised reforms by the Concert of Europe and so often abandoned to the revenges of the Ottoman Government—as well as the Cilician highlands and some outlet to the sea." To these provinces will naturally be added the Armenian territory acquired by Russia.

The question as to whether there are still enough survivors to populate such a state can most fortunately, in spite of the repeated attempts at national annihilation, be answered in the affirmative. It will not be necessary for us to lean wholly upon the noble suggestion offered by M. Paul Doumer, late President of the French Senate, who recently said that should lack of numbers be urged by the enemy as an obstacle to an independent Armenian state "the dead must be counted with the living." The paucity of numbers is not so dire as to endanger in any way the Armenian hope. When Greece finally achieved her liberation from the Turkish yoke her numbers had been reduced to about 500,000, and Serbia and Bulgaria were equally decimated when they achieved theirs; and yet these states have stood and their populations have multiplied. Armenia, with the Russian provinces, with Persia, and with the Dispersion to draw upon, together with the refugees in the Caucasus, Mesopotamia, Egypt and Palestine, and the Armenians of Constantinople and Smyrna, who have in general been spared, is numerically in a stronger position than were any of the Balkan states. To defraud the Armenians of their independence because of the losses they have sustained, or for any other reason, would be not only to commit a monstrous outrage, but actually to accomplish the very end designed by their arch enemies,—to drain the brimming cup of their long sacrifice in company with these criminals. This the world will never consent to do, and it is with a high hope of a just and complete deliverance that Armenia will present herself at the World Court.

It will not be the first time that this Figure has presented itself before an International Congress. But whereas in the past she came as an unknown supplicator, as an alien champion of a long forgotten cause—still in her quaint Crusader's dress—to throw herself, alas, in vain, upon the chivalry of the Great Powers, her sisters in religion and race; one marvels to record, that tomorrow she will come, her unsurrendered cross still upon her breast, as defender-at-arms of the victorious cause of World Democracy,—its last defender at the farthest outpost of the field of war in that long embattled region: a mysterious figure still, like one risen from the dead: a nation without a state, without navy, and even without army in the ordinary sense, a nation whose banner is scarcely known to any but her own children; and yet the nation which, in proportion to numbers and resources, has paid the highest impost of life and treasure in the whole gigantic conflict. But for all the heroism of her gallant, her exalted sons and daughters she will wear no sword. In her right hand there will be a higher symbol of her might— the palm of her long martyrdom.

Will the nations assembled there understand the full significance of this sublime Figure as she makes her plea for justice? Will they defend her from the Powers of Chaos and Darkness which have sought to destroy her in their rapacious desire to possess themselves of her inheritance? Will they uphold the spiritual verities of which she is the symbol, and in the perfect triumph of which alone lies the peace and safety of the world?

Armenia will seek no crown or sceptre, nor will there be in her eyes the fire of revenge or lust for conquest. As throughout her history, so will she still aspire for freedom, for culture, for progress and for peace,—for all that man holds good. The nations of the world, assembled in that great Council, will surely at last understand the grandeur, the pity and the meaning of her sacrifice, and by setting the seal of their approval upon her aspirations for democracy and light, they will indeed pay grateful tribute to the memory of her martyrs and bear testimony to their faith in the ideals for which those martyrs died.

NOTES

NOTE 1

The Aryan origin of the Armenian race is recognized by all authorities. We are indebted to Herodotus for the specific story of their former connection with Europe. He says that the Armenians are a branch of the Phrygians. The Phrygians, according to tradition, before their migration to Asia lived in the neighborhood of Macedonia. Strabo makes a statement which suggests an even more picturesque origin when he says that Armen, a native of Armenion, a city of Thessaly, sailed in company with Jason toward the country afterwards named for him. Rawlinson seems to be the only authority who does not trace the Armenians to Europe. His theory is that Armenia itself was the original home of the Aryan peoples. The foundation for their own tradition that they are descendants of Thorkom, or Togarmah, a grandson of Japhet, may, for want of historical evidence, remain forever merely a matter for interesting speculation.

NOTE 2

In one of the earlier chapters of "The Beginnings of New England," Mr. Fiske, speaking of "the first bold and determined manifestation of the Protestant temper of revolt against spiritual despotism," says:

"From Armenia in the ninth century the Manichæan

sect of Paulicians came into Thrace and for twenty generations played a considerable part in the history of the Eastern Empire. They were known in Bulgaria as Bogomiles. In the Greek tongue they were called Cathari, or 'Puritans.' . . .

"Their ecclesiastical government was in the main Presbyterian, and in politics they showed a decided leaning toward democracy. They wore long faces, looked askance at frivolous amusements, and were terribly in earnest. Of the more obscure pages of mediæval history, none are fuller of interest than those in which we decipher the westward progress of these sturdy heretics, through the Balkan peninsula into Italy, and thence into Southern France, where, toward the end of the twelfth century, we find their ideas coming to full bloom in the great Albigensian heresy. . . . After forty years of slaughter, these Albigensian Cathari or Puritans seemed exterminated, but the spirit of revolt against the hierarchy continued to live on obscurely, ready on occasion to spring into fresh and vigorous life. . . . This Protestant reformation, from the thirteenth century to the nineteenth, is coincident with the transfer of the world's political center of gravity from the Tiber and Rhine to the Thames and the Mississippi."

Referring to Armenian Protestantism, the late Dr. Robert Chambers of Western Turkey Mission, writing in the *Missionary Herald* makes the following interesting statement: "Some of the first to discover and attach themselves to the American missionaries in the early part of the last century in Armenia were descendants of the Armenian Paulicians."

Note 3

Research on Armenian art is still in its infancy. Even the manuscript literature has not yet been fully studied. Of the art of illuminating, which advanced to a high degree of skill and beauty in the Middle Ages, we know comparatively little, although it is beginning to be made the object of special study by certain modern scholars. The gold and silversmiths' art, said to have attained its height in the tenth century, has continued to find fascinating and original expression even to recent days. I have seen an exquisite silver handleless cup, made by an artisan of the city of Van, famous for its silversmiths, which exhibited evidence of marked genius. It was covered with very chaste, minute, and delicately wrought geometric designs. In the center, supported by a pivot, was a fish, covered with carven scales and very flexible, which, when the cup was filled with liquid, seemed to swim. A very suggestive article upon the subject of Armenian decorative art may be found in the International Encyclopedia.

Note 4

With regard to the physique of the Armenians we have much enlightening testimony from persons who have traveled and lived among them. The veteran missionary, Dr. Joseph K. Greene, author of "Leavening the Levant," attributes their survival as a people to their physical, no less than to their moral vigor:

"The first reason of their survival," he says, "is that the Armenians inhabited, not the hot and feverish plains of Mesopotamia but the broad and elevated plateau of northeastern Asia Minor. Even as far south as Van, their ancient capital, their country was 5,500 feet above sea level, with the snow-capped peak of Ararat only one hundred miles to the northeast. Like the inhabitants of the Caucasus—the Circassians—they were a ruddy, vigorous, healthy race. Their land was fertile and produced fine cereals and fruits, with abounding flocks and herds. Theirs was a life of toil, a perpetual fight with nature, but they breathed pure air and were well fed. Hence the Armenians were a hardy and handsome race, and were capable of great endurance."

Even when subjected to the trials of migration, they continue to preserve their aspect of physical well being. Some twelve or more years ago, I heard that veteran orator, the late Mary A. Livermore, open an address to an audience of Armenians assembled in Faneuil Hall, Boston, with the following striking but very seriously spoken words: "This is the handsomest audience I have ever stood before." I myself have never addressed an Armenian audience without receiving an impression of their morally illuminated vitality. And frequently after lectures to American audiences, school teachers have come up to me to express both their admiration and love for the beautiful Armenian children in their care, and their indignation that such splendid human material should be so recklessly wasted.

NOTE 5

I cannot let the occasion pass without paying my personal tribute to the really chivalrous men and women in Europe and America who have consecrated themselves to the Armenian cause. The names of Gladstone, Bryce, Dillon, Lynch, Zangwill, MacColl, the Duke of Argyle, Hamlin, Christie, Greene, Chambers, Barton, Usher, Yarrow, Knapp, Trowbridge, Shattuck, Wheeler, Townsend, Leroy-Beaulieu, Berard, Anatole France, Jaurès, Clémenceau, Pressensé, Quillard, de Contenson, de Roberty, Rolin-Jaquemyns, Favre, Blackwell, Barrows, Howe, Clement, Garrison, Storey, Ames, Mead, Dole, and others whose names will suggest themselves to those familiar with this history, are destined to be immortally linked with the names of the Armenian patriots and to glorify the walls of the future Armenian Pantheon.

NOTE 6

The fact that only two years later America rescued Cuba from the tyranny of Spain is proof in itself that had she not been, in a way, inhibited by her traditional policy of non-interference in European affairs, she would have flown to arms in defense of Armenia, regardless of the fact that she was under no "treaty" obligations whatever. Had she been true to the vision of her prophets, she would, even as it was, have taken that step, and by assuming the rôle of moral leadership which she now enjoys, have added to her own spiritual force the strength of popular England, France, Italy, and who knows what other countries.

Note 7

Is it anything more than a coincidence that the persecution of the Jews in Russia took on at this time the violent character of earlier days—that Kishinef and Kief followed Van, Ourfa, and Sassoun?

Note 8

Even now, the privilege of acquaintance with some of the works of these, and others of the poets, is available through Miss Blackwell's admirable translations which appear in a volume entitled "Armenian Poems," now on sale at the office of the Armenian and Syrian Relief Committee at 3 Joy Street, Boston. The price of this book is $1.00 and the entire proceeds are devoted by Miss Blackwell to the Relief Fund.

Note 9

The genuineness of the Armenian desire to co-operate with the Turks in the new government is testified to by all foreigners who were in Turkey at the time of the Proclamation. One of these, Mr. Herbert Adams Gibbons, author of "The New Map of Europe," etc., remarks, concerning both the antecedents and consequences of the "revolution," that the Young Turk agitators had been encouraged and even sometimes supported by Armenians, who "took them in, fed them and clothed them and subsidized their propaganda."

"I was present at the overthrow of the Hamidian régime," he writes. "I saw the Young Turk exiles returning triumphant to Constantinople and Smyrna and

Beirut. I saw Mohammedan Mullahs and Ulema fraternize with Armenian priests. I saw them riding in carriages together. I saw them kiss Christians on the cheeks and call them brothers. Then, immediately, remorselessly, and without hesitation the Young Turks turned on those who had helped them and whom they had used to bring about the Revolution. Not many months of the new régime had passed before we who were on the ground in Turkey realized that there was absolutely no difference between Young Turks and Old Turks. By 'peace and liberty' the Young Turks meant peace and liberty for Moslems—and not even for all Moslems! Albanian and Arab Moslems were given to understand as fully as Armenians and Greeks and Syrians and Jews that Turkey was Turkish."

Note 10

For this document and for the information contained in the paragraph which follows it, as well as for other material, I am indebted to Mr. Mikaël Varandian's excellent book, "L'Arménie et la Question Arménienne."

Note 11

I have taken the description of the cartoon in "Karagöz" verbatim from "Armenia and the War" by Mr. A. P. Hacobian of London. To his moving and able presentation, I also owe other material as well as much inspiration.

Note 12

Mr. A. P. Hacobian, in his book "Armenia and the War," quotes the following from the *Retch,* organ of the

Constitutional Democrats in Russia, issue of July 28, 1916 (O. S.):

"The scheme of settling Russian emigrants in the occupied parts of Turkish Armenia, recently discussed in the Duma, is being energetically carried out. This matter has been the subject of a lively discussion between the Emigration and Military authorities. Investigations are in progress, not only in the districts near the frontier, but also further afield, the fertile Mush valley being the object of special attention. Agricultural Battalions have been in course of organization since last autumn and already number 5,000 men. More will be found presently. *Armenians and Georgians are excluded.* The task of these young arms is to cultivate the fields on which investigations have been carried out, under the supervision of agricultural experts, in order to facilitate the provisioning of the army. The question of emigrating the families of these men is also under consideration.

"Side by side with this scheme there exists another scheme of settling Cossacks in Turkish Armenia, on similar lines to what has already been done in Northern Caucasus with good results. *Those who have conceived these schemes have in view the creation of a sufficiently broad zone inhabited by Russians, separating the Russian Armenians from the Turkish Armenians.*

"Armenian refugees are gradually returning to their country and resuming the work of cultivating their lands. They usually settle in the villages that have suffered least, their own villages having been totally ruined.

"To avoid confusion, the Grand Duke Nicholas

issued a Ukase in March last, warning these returned refugees to keep themselves in readiness to vacate these districts on the establishment of Russian Civil Administration. In the same Ukase the Commander-in-Chief of the Caucasian Army has decreed that the vacant lands in the plains of Alashkert, Diadin and Bayazid may be given in hire up to the time of the return of their rightful owners. *General Yudenitch has issued orders, however, prohibiting the settlement in these places of any other immigrants except Russians and Cossacks.* Only those natives are permitted to return who are able to prove ownership of land or property by legal documents. This arrangement makes it impossible for the natives (Armenians) to return to their homes because it is ridiculous to speak of title-deeds when dealing with land in Turkey; and as for other documents which prove ownership, these always get lost during flight.

"In the above three plains, also in parts of the plain of Bassain, the surviving native inhabitants are debarred from returning to their homes and resuming their peaceful occupations."

Note 13

The complicity of the German government with that of the Turk in the crime against the Armenians is evident even on the face of things, since the Turks would not have dared to work in opposition to the will of their masters. Nor could they have secured the active co-operation of the German officers in Turkey had there not been strict accord between them. Such a statement as this by Signor Gorrini, in the interview already referred to, is typical of many directly corroborative statements made by foreign and other eye-witnesses who were in Turkey during the perpetration of the crime: " . . . the Germans and the Committee (of Union of Progress) constitute the one genuine, solid organization at present existing in Turkey—a masterly and most rigorous organization, which does not hesitate to use any weapon whatever; an organization of audacity, of terror, and of mysterious, ferocious revenge."

BIBLIOGRAPHY

For information concerning Armenian history, the Armenian question, the Near Eastern question, travel in Armenia, Armenia in the War, Armenian history and art, the reader is referred to the following works, to which the author wishes to acknowledge her indebtedness.

In English:

THE HISTORY OF VARTAN, AND OF THE BATTLE OF THE ARMENIANS: AN ACCOUNT OF THE RELIGIOUS WARS BETWEEN THE PERSIANS AND ARMENIANS, by Elisæus, Bishop of the Amadunians. Translated from the Armenian by C. F. Neumann. London, 1830.

HISTORY OF ARMENIA, by Father Michael Chamich. Translated from the original Armenian by Johannes Avdall. Calcutta, 1827.

RESEARCHES IN ARMENIA, by E. Smith. Boston, 1833.

TRAVELS AND RESEARCHES IN MESOPOTAMIA AND ARMENIA, by W. F. Ainsworth. London, 1842.

TRAVELS IN ARMENIA, by A. H. Layard. London, 1853.

THE ARMENIAN CHURCH—HISTORY, LITURGY, DOCTRINES AND CEREMONIES, by E. F. Fortescue. London, J. T. Hayes, 1872.

ARMENIA AND THE ARMENIANS, by R. D. J. Issaverdens. Venice, 1878.

LIFE AND ADVENTURES IN TREBIZOND, ERZERUM, TABRIZ, by A. Vambéry. London, 1886.

ARMENIA AND THE CAMPAIGN OF 1877, by C. B. Norman. London, 1878.

THE ARMENIANS, OR THE PEOPLE OF ARARAT, by M. C. Gabrielian. Allen, Lane & Scott, Philadelphia, 1892.

TWENTY YEARS OF THE ARMENIAN QUESTION, by James Bryce, in his TRANSCAUCASIA AND ARARAT, pp. 446-525. 1890.

ARMENIA AND THE ARMENIANS, by E. J. Dillon (a section in his RUSSIAN CHARACTERISTICS).

THE RULE OF THE TURK, by Frederick D. Greene. Putnam, New York, 1896.

TURKEY AND THE ARMENIAN ATROCITIES, by E. M. Bliss.

ENGLAND'S RESPONSIBILITY TOWARD ARMENIA, by Malcolm McColl. Longmans, London, 1895.

THROUGH ARMENIA ON HORSEBACK, by George H. Hepworth. Dutton, New York, 1898.

ARMENIA: TRAVELS AND STUDIES, by H. F. B. Lynch. Longmans Green, London, 1901.

THE ARMENIAN AWAKENING: A HISTORY OF THE ARMENIAN CHURCH, by Leon Arpee. University of Chicago Press, 1909.

ON THE CROSS OF EUROPE'S IMPERIALISM: ARMENIA CRUCIFIED, by Diana A. Apcar. Fukuin Printing Co., Yokohama, 1918.

THE TREATMENT OF ARMENIANS IN THE OTTOMAN EMPIRE, 1915-16. Documents presented to Viscount Grey by Viscount Bryce, with a preface by Viscount Bryce. English Blue Book, London, 1916.

ARMENIAN ATROCITIES: THE MURDER OF A NATION, by Arnold J. Toynbee. Hodder & Stoughton, London, 1915.

THE BLACKEST PAGE OF MODERN HISTORY; EVENTS IN ARMENIA IN 1915, THE FACTS AND THE RESPONSIBILITIES, by Herbert Adams Gibbons. Putnam, New York and London, 1916.

THE STORY OF THE ARMENIAN DYNASTIES, by James L. Barton. *The Independent,* March 5th, 1899.

THE RECONSTRUCTION OF POLAND AND THE NEAR EAST; PROBLEMS OF PEACE, by Herbert Adams Gibbons. Century, New York, 1917.

ARMENIA AND THE WAR, by A. P. Hacobian, with a preface by Viscount Bryce. Hodder & Stoughton, London and New York, 1917.

THE TURKISH EMPIRE: ITS GROWTH AND DECAY, by Lord Eversley. Dodd, Mead & Co., New York, 1917.

TRAVEL AND POLITICS IN ARMENIA, by Noel E. Buxton and Harold J. Buxton, with an introduction by Viscount Bryce and a contribution on Armenian History and Culture by Aram Raffi. Smith, Elder & Co., London, 1914.

ARMENIA PAST AND PRESENT: A STUDY AND A FORECAST, by W. L. Williams, with an introduction by T. P. O'Connor, M. P. P. S. King & Son, Ltd., London, 1916.

THE PAN-GERMAN PLOT UNMASKED, by André Chéradame, with an introduction by the Earl of Cromer. Scribners, London, 1917.

TWO WAR YEARS IN CONSTANTINOPLE: SKETCHES OF GERMAN AND YOUNG TURKISH ETHICS AND POLITICS, by

Harry Stuermer. Translated from the German by E. Allen and the author. Doran, New York, 1917.

THE WAR AND THE BAGDAD RAILWAY: THE STORY OF ASIA MINOR AND ITS RELATION TO THE PRESENT CONFLICT, by Morris Jastrow, Jr. Lippincott, 1917.

THE NEAR EAST FROM WITHIN, anonymous. Dutton, New York, 1918.

THE GOLDEN MAIDEN AND OTHER FOLK AND FAIRY TALES TOLD IN ARMENIA, by A. G. Seklemian, with an introduction by Alice Stone Blackwell. Helman Taylor Co., Cleveland, O., 1898.

ARMENIAN POEMS, rendered into English verse by Alice Stone Blackwell. Armenian Relief Comm., 3 Joy St., Boston, 1917.

ARMENIAN LEGENDS AND POEMS, compiled and illustrated by Zabelle C. Boyajian. With an introduction by Viscount Bryce, and a contribution on Armenia, its Epics, Folk Songs and Mediæval Poetry by Aram Raffi. Dent, London, 1916.

ARMENIAN LITERATURE, with an introduction by Robert Arnot. Revised Edition, London, 1901.

ARMENIAN POEMS: Metrical Version, by Robert Arnot. London, 1901.

In French:

HISTOIRE D'ARMÉNIE, by Moses de Khoren. Translated from ancient Armenian by P. E. Le Vaillant de Florival. Venice, 1841.

L'ARMÉNIE ET LA QUESTION ARMÉNIENNE, by Mikaël Varandian. With a preface by Victor Bérard. Kavanagh et Cie, Laval, France, 1917.

CONTES ARMÉNIENS, TRADUITS DE L'ARMÉNIEN MODERNE, by Frédéric Macler. Leroux, Paris, 1903.

MEKHITARISTES DE SAINT LAZARE, HISTOIRE D'ARMÉNIE, LITTÉRATURE ARMÉNIENNE, by Paul Emile Le Vaillant de Florival. Typographié Arménienne de Saint Lazare, Venice.

L'ARMÉNIE CHRÉTIENNE ET SA LITTÉRATURE, by Felix Neve. C. Peters, Louvain, 1886.

L'ARMÉNIE, SON HISTOIRE, SA LITTÉRATURE, SON RÔLE EN L'ORIENT, with an Introduction by Anatole France, by Archag Tchobanian. Société du Mercure de France, Paris, 1897.

POÈMES ARMÉNIENS, ANCIENS ET MODERNES, Precedés d'une Etude de Gabriel Mourey sur la Poésie et l'Art Arméniens, by Archag Tchobanian. Librairie A. Charles, 1902.

CHANTS POPULAIRES ARMÉNIENS, Préface de Paul Adam, by Archag Tchobanian. Société d'Editions Littéraires et Artistiques, Paris, 1903.

PETITE BIBLIOTHÈQUE ARMÉNIENNE, Publiée sous la Direction de Frédéric Macler. Paris.

L'ORIENT INÉDIT—LEGENDES ET TRADITIONS ARMÉNIENNES, by Minas Tcheraz. Leroux, Paris, 1912.

ETUDES SUR LA MINIATURE ARMÉNIENNE, by Seraphin Abdullah and Frédéric Macler, Paris, 1909.

AU MILIEU DES MASSACRES—JOURNAL DE LA FEMME D'UN CONSUL DE FRANCE EN ARMÉNIE, by Emilie Carlier Juven, Paris, 1903.

Also to the following journals: *The New Armenia*, 949 Broadway, New York; *The Armenian Herald*, Old

South Building, Boston; *La Voix de l'Arménie,* 30 Rue Jacob, Paris.

(A complete bibliography of the Armenian disasters, compiled by Prof. W. W. Rockwell, may be had from the American Committee for Armenian Relief, One Madison Avenue, New York City, price 10 cents.)

Fastback Titles *(continued from back cover)*

107. Fostering a Pluralistic Society Through Multi-Ethnic Education
108. Education and the Brain
109. Bonding: The First Basic in Education
110. Selecting Instructional Materials
111. Teacher Improvement Through Clinical Supervision
112. Places and Spaces: Environmental Psychology in Education
113. Artists as Teachers
114. Using Role Playing in the Classroom
115. Management by Objectives in the Schools
116. Declining Enrollments: A New Dilemma for Educators
117. Teacher Centers—Where, What, Why?
118. The Case for Competency-Based Education
119. Teaching the Gifted and Talented
120. Parents Have Rights, Too!
121. Student Discipline and the Law
122. British Schools and Ours
123. Church-State Issues in Education
124. Mainstreaming: Merging Regular and Special Education
125. Early Field Experiences in Teacher Education
126. Student and Teacher Absenteeism
127. Writing Centers in the Elementary School
128. A Primer on Piaget
129. The Restoration of Standards: The Modesto Plan
130. Dealing with Stress: A Challenge for Educators
131. Futuristics and Education
132. How Parent-Teacher Conferences Build Partnerships
133. Early Childhood Education: Foundations for Lifelong Learning
134. Teaching about the Creation/Evolution Controversy
135. Performance Evaluation of Educational Personnel
136. Writing for Education Journals
137. Minimum Competency Testing
138. Legal Implications of Minimum Competency Testing
139. Energy Education: Goals and Practices
140. Education in West Germany: A Quest for Excellence
141. Magnet Schools: An Approach to Voluntary Desegregation
142. Intercultural Education
143. The Process of Grant Proposal Development
144. Citizenship and Consumer Education: Key Assumptions and Basic Competencies
145. Migrant Education: Teaching the Wandering Ones
146. Controversial Issues in Our Schools
147. Nutrition and Learning
148. Education in the USSR
149. Teaching with Newspapers: The Living Curriculum
150. Population, Education, and Children's Futures
151. Bibliotherapy: The Right Book at the Right Time
152. Educational Planning for Educational Success
153. Questions and Answers on Moral Education
154. Mastery Learning
155. The Third Wave and Education's Futures
156. Title IX: Implications for Education of Women
157. Elementary Mathematics: Priorities for the 1980s
158. Summer School: A New Look
159. Education for Cultural Pluralism: Global Roots Stew
160. Pluralism Gone Mad
161. Education Agenda for the 1980s
162. The Public Community College: The People's University
163. Technology in Education: Its Human Potential
164. Children's Books: A Legacy for the Young
165. Teacher Unions and the Power Structure
166. Progressive Education: Lessons from Three Schools
167. Basic Education: A Historical Perspective
168. Aesthetic Education and the Quality of Life
169. Teaching the Learning Disabled
170. Safety Education in the Elementary School
171. Education in Contemporary Japan
172. The School's Role in the Prevention of Child Abuse
173. Death Education: A Concern for the Living
174. Youth Participation for Early Adolescents: Learning and Serving in the Community
175. Time Management for Educators
176. Educating Verbally Gifted Youth
177. Beyond Schooling: Education in a Broader Context
178. New Audiences for Teacher Education
179. Microcomputers in the Classroom
180. Supervision Made Simple
181. Educating Older People: Another View of Mainstreaming
182. School Public Relations: Communicating to the Community
183. Economic Education Across the Curriculum
184. Using the Census as a Creative Teaching Resource

Single copies of fastbacks are 75¢ (60¢ to Phi Delta Kappa members). Write to Phi Delta Kappa, Eighth and Union, Box 789, Bloomington, IN 47402 **for quantity discounts for any title or combination of titles.**

PDK Fastback Series Titles

1. Schools Without Property Taxes: Hope or Illusion?
3. Open Education: Promise and Problems
4. Performance Contracting: Who Profits Most?
6. How Schools Can Apply Systems Analysis
7. Busing: A Moral Issue
8. Discipline or Disaster?
9. Learning Systems for the Future
10. Who Should Go to College?
11. Alternative Schools in Action
12. What Do Students Really Want?
13. What Should the Schools Teach?
14. How to Achieve Accountability in the Public Schools
15. Needed: A New Kind of Teacher
17. Systematic Thinking about Education
18. Selecting Children's Reading
19. Sex Differences in Learning to Read
20. Is Creativity Teachable?
21. Teachers and Politics
22. The Middle School: Whence? What? Whither?
23. Publish: Don't Perish
26. The Teacher and the Drug Scene
29. Can Intelligence Be Taught?
30. How to Recognize a Good School
31. In Between: The Adolescent's Struggle for Independence
32. Effective Teaching in the Desegregated School
34. Leaders Live with Crises
35. Marshalling Community Leadership to Support the Public Schools
36. Preparing Educational Leaders: New Challenges and New Perspectives
37. General Education: The Search for a Rationale
38. The Humane Leader
39. Parliamentary Procedure: Tool of Leadership
40. Aphorisms on Education
41. Metrication, American Style
42. Optional Alternative Public Schools
43. Motivation and Learning in School
44. Informal Learning
45. Learning Without a Teacher
46. Violence in the Schools: Causes and Remedies
47. The School's Responsibility for Sex Education
48. Three Views of Competency-Based Teacher Education: I Theory
49. Three Views of Competency-Based Teacher Education: II University of Houston
50. Three Views of Competency-Based Teacher Education: III University of Nebraska
51. A University for the World: The United Nations Plan
52. Oikos, the Environment and Education
53. Transpersonal Psychology in Education
56. Equity in School Financing: Full State Funding
57. Equity in School Financing: District Power Equalizing
58. The Computer in the School
59. The Legal Rights of Students
60. The Word Game: Improving Communications
61. Planning the Rest of Your Life
62. The People and Their Schools: Community Participation
63. The Battle of the Books: Kanawha County
64. The Community as Textbook
65. Students Teach Students
66. The Pros and Cons of Ability Grouping
67. A Conservative Alternative School: The A+ School in Cupertino
68. How Much Are Our Young People Learning? The Story of the National Assessment
69. Diversity in Higher Education: Reform in the Colleges
70. Dramatics in the Classroom: Making Lessons Come Alive
72. Alternatives to Growth: Education for a Stable Society
73. Thomas Jefferson and the Education of a New Nation
74. Three Early Champions of Education: Benjamin Franklin, Benjamin Rush, and Noah Webster
76. The American Teacher: 1776-1976
77. The Urban School Superintendency: A Century and a Half of Change
78. Private Schools: From the Puritans to the Present
79. The People and Their Schools
80. Schools of the Past: A Treasury of Photographs
81. Sexism: New Issue in American Education
82. Computers in the Curriculum
83. The Legal Rights of Teachers
84. Learning in Two Languages
84S. Learning in Two Languages (Spanish edition)
85. Getting It All Together: Confluent Education
86. Silent Language in the Classroom
87. Multiethnic Education: Practices and Promises
88. How a School Board Operates
89. What Can We Learn from the Schools of China?
90. Education in South Africa
91. What I've Learned About Values Education
92. The Abuses of Standardized Testing
93. The Uses of Standardized Testing
94. What the People Think About Their Schools: Gallup's Findings
95. Defining the Basics of American Education
96. Some Practical Laws of Learning
97. Reading 1967-1977: A Decade of Change and Promise
98. The Future of Teacher Power in America
99. Collective Bargaining in the Public Schools
100. How to Individualize Learning
101. Winchester: A Community School for the Urbanvantaged
102. Affective Education in Philadelphia
103. Teaching with Film
104. Career Education: An Open Door Policy
105. The Good Mind
106. Law in the Curriculum

(Continued on inside back cover)

See inside back cover for prices.